Member's Manual

Your Guide to a Christ-Centered Program

PARACLETE PRESS
BREWSTER, MASSACHUSETTS

Revised and Updated January, 1998

Published by Paraclete Press
Brewster, Massachusetts
www.paraclete-press.com

Printed in the United States of America.

Welcome to 3D!

After 25 years, through the support of the 3D program half a million men and women have found spiritual growth, weight loss and new life. The 3D support group is a safe place where members face their feelings, their fears and their conflicts honestly—and they are healed. This is why enthusiasm for 3D has been so contagious. It works! It helps members learn to walk through the stresses of daily living.

As 3D becomes part of your life style, we encourage you to be obedient in three areas: in your diet, in your daily devotions, and in being open, honest and vulnerable in your group. God wants to establish a new work in your life. That's why ongoing attendance at 3D group meetings is so important. Yes, God honors commitment and obedience.

After you have completed the first twelve weeks, you should continue to go on to session two. In the first twelve weeks you will begin to feel the difference and look forward to your weekly meetings. The structure is more flexible after you have completed your initial twelve-week session, but every meeting you attend will be rewarding. The 3D devotional *Devotions for Daily Living* will provide you with readings for 36 additional weeks, whether in a group or in your personal reading. We encourage 3D'ers to stay connected—check in with a group whenever you can. Over the years you will find this gives you support to maintain not only the weight loss, but the transparency, neediness and trust in God which brings real peace and joy.

Maintaining an ongoing 3D support group in your church enables you to attend a group and grow year after year. Churches that use 3D as a yearly curriculum discover it to be a powerful tool for both outreach and Christian growth.

May every day in 3D be the beginning of the greatest adventure of your life!

3D Benefits

Physical
- ❏ A well-balanced diet program from the American Dietetic and Diabetic Association.
- ❏ The use of daily exercise to promote the well-being of God's temple—your body.

Spiritual
- ❏ Bible readings and questions.
- ❏ Daily devotional readings.
- ❏ Scripture memorization.
- ❏ Growth, both individually and as a group.

Emotional
- ❏ Understanding yourself better.
- ❏ Sharing through small groups that meet weekly.
- ❏ Caring for others.

Social
- ❏ Reaching out within churches, neighborhoods, and communities.
- ❏ Getting to know people of different ages and backgrounds.
- ❏ Learning to be at ease with yourself and with others.

We believe this program will provide the ABCs you need to become a better you!

Begin with anticipation! God bless you as you begin this new adventure!

Table of Contents

Diet

Healthy Eating

The diet part of this program introduces you to a plan for sensible eating habits. 3D has successfully helped over half a million people learn the value of good eating. Healthy eating has become an increasing need in our society where fast foods have become a daily habit instead of a treat once in a while. We find ourselves "driving through" to get our breakfast, lunch, or dinner on our way to something else. Family meal time happens only once or twice a week instead of daily.

God has always used the area of food to teach his people truth about themselves and about him. The Garden of Eden is our first introduction to the individual wanting to do "his/her" own thing when it came to eating! "I want what I want when I want it" is the cry that came out of the garden and is still the cry of most of us when it comes to food.

The manna from heaven was provided by God to show his people that he did care about their hunger, and that he would indeed take care of them. But soon the manna didn't satisfy (does that sound familiar?). Then, of course, throughout the life of Jesus many of his miracles centered around food—the feeding of the 5,000, the wedding feast at Cana and others. His teaching often occurred around the table—with Martha and Mary, with Zaccheus, and of course with his disciples. Jesus' very life is given to us by our receiving the bread and wine in Communion. And, at the end of life, we have all been invited to the banquet table with him. Food is woven in and out of the Bible with great significance, and it is woven in and out of our lives today in much the same way.

Food, like everything else, needs to come under the Lordship of Christ, and we need to walk towards that goal. The whole area of food brings out rebellion, fear, and anxiousness, and it reveals a lot about who we are inside (which is exactly what happened in the Bible!).

In 3D we are concerned with sound nutrition and well-balanced meals, and we would like to thank Pamela Saltsman, MPHRD for her contribution to this revised edition of the Member's Manual. We have used the ADA (American Dietetic Association) diet as the basis of our program. The calories have already been counted and the individual is taught about the basic food groups and about how to exchange foods within groups. Once you learn the ADA diet, it is always a part of your thinking.

If you have joined a group for the purpose of losing weight, we believe the ADA diet is a medically sound diet plan. If you have joined to get help with anorexia nervosa and need to gain weight, we also believe the ADA plan is the best instruction you can receive to help you with your eating disorder. If you have joined any group sponsored by 3D and are not at all interested in dieting, please consider acquainting yourself with this plan. We believe it will be a tremendous blessing to you and your family and will be a real aid to better health.

Looking at food with the following exchange lists in mind is a new experience, and it takes practice to become familiar with them. So don't be discouraged, and do allow time for menu planning.

The 3D program emphasizes good nutrition, proper eating habits and sensible weight loss. While you are in this program, the whole family can benefit from well balanced meals and will develop good eating habits. They can eat all the same foods you do, adding extras like larger servings or sauces.

3D's Dietitian

Loretta Jack, R.D., is a Registered Dietitian with the American Dietetic Association. Ms. Jack has a Bachelor of Science degree from Cornell University in food and nutrition. She completed her dietetic internship at Massachusetts General Hospital. For nine years she continued to work there, first as a staff therapeutic dietitian, and then as unit co-ordinator for the medical building. In addition, Ms. Jack has served as treasurer of the Massachusetts Dietetic Association, as well as co-chairman of its Dial-A-Dietitian program. She joined the 3D staff as a consultant in 1980.

Charting Your Course

As you consider what your weight is and what you want it to be, do remember that the following charts and equations are only guidelines, and that you should prayerfully consider what is right for you.

Many people have strong feelings about what their ideal weight is, but their opinion may differ from what is right for them. For example, a person who has lost weight may wish to continue to the point where he or she becomes excessively thin. Then it is important for someone to help the person examine whatever feelings may be underneath this desire.

By using the Harris-Benedict equation on page 14, you can adjust your daily caloric intake to meet your weight loss or weight maintenance needs. Once you have determined how many calories you need to eat each day, find the exchanges for this number of calories in the chart on the Model Meal Plan (see page 19). Watch your weight carefully, although not obsessively, as you begin the new diet. Each person's body reacts differently, and further adjustments may be needed.

One advantage of the 3D diet is that it trains members in proper eating habits. Eating habits developed during weight loss (or weight gain) are the basis for the disciplined eating which should continue throughout life.

As members begin a maintenance regimen, they will continue to learn how they can manage their food intake so they won't gain back the weight they lost. Members will learn how many extras they can have or how much larger their portions can be. Even on maintenance regimen the same good habits of low-fat, high-fiber eating will be reinforced.

Lactating and pregnant women should check with their doctor before beginning any diet program.

What's the Right Weight?

Ideal body weight differs for each person. Each person has her or his own unique body composition based on body frame and distribution of fat and muscle. The location and amount of fat are sometimes better predictors than actual body weight for determining a person's health risk. For example, a muscular person may seem to be overweight according to weight charts. But, because muscle weighs more than fat, the person may actually be at his proper weight.

The Body Mass Index or BMI is a standard measurement that researchers use to assess obesity. You can calculate your BMI by dividing your weight (in kilograms) by your height (in meters) squared. Or use the chart below to estimate your BMI.

Height	Body Mass Index (BMI)													
	19	20	21	22	23	24	25	26	27	28	29	30	35	40
	Weight (pounds)													
4'10"	91	96	100	105	110	115	119	124	129	134	138	143	167	191
4'11"	94	99	104	109	114	119	124	128	133	138	143	148	173	198
5'0"	97	102	107	112	118	123	128	133	138	143	148	153	179	204
5'1"	100	106	111	116	122	127	132	137	143	148	153	158	185	211
5'2"	104	109	115	120	126	131	136	142	147	153	158	164	191	218
5'3"	107	113	118	124	130	135	141	146	152	158	163	169	197	225
5'4"	110	116	122	128	134	140	145	151	157	163	169	174	204	232
5'5"	114	120	126	132	138	144	150	156	162	168	174	180	210	240
5'6"	118	124	130	136	142	148	155	161	167	173	179	186	216	247
5'7"	121	127	134	140	146	153	159	166	172	178	185	191	223	255
5'8"	125	131	138	144	151	158	164	171	177	184	190	197	230	262
5'9"	128	135	142	149	155	162	169	176	182	189	196	203	236	270
5'10"	132	139	146	153	160	167	174	181	188	195	202	207	243	278
5'11"	136	143	150	157	165	172	179	186	193	200	208	215	250	286
6'0"	140	147	154	162	169	177	184	191	199	206	213	221	258	294
6'1"	144	151	159	166	174	182	189	197	204	212	219	227	265	302
6'2"	148	155	163	171	179	186	194	202	210	218	225	233	272	311
6'3"	152	160	168	176	184	192	200	208	216	224	232	240	279	319
6'4"	156	164	172	180	189	197	205	213	221	230	238	246	287	328
							OVERWEIGHT					OBESE		

Source: World Health Organization

The American Institute for Cancer Research (AICR) recommends that people maintain a BMI between 18.5 and 25 throughout their life. The AICR also suggests that people do not gain more than eleven pounds throughout their adult life. Those people with a BMI above 25 are usually defined as "overweight" and those above 30 as "obese."

The BMI overall is a good guideline for determining whether a person is within his or her ideal body weight. However, the BMI is not a good indicator for fat distribution. Therefore, even if your BMI is in a healthy range you may benefit from losing a little weight because your body fat may still be too high. People who have a higher distribution of fat around the chest or belly areas versus their hips and thighs have a higher risk for disease. One way to know if you are carrying excess body fat is through the Waist to Hip ratio.

To determine your Waste to Hip ratio simply divide your waist measurement by your hip measurement. For women, your waist to hip measurement should be at or below 0.85 and for men, 0.95.

How to Set Your Course

You may compute your Daily Caloric Need following the guidelines on these pages. How many calories people require is based on many factors including their age, height, present weight, and activity level.

Your Basal Energy Expenditure (BEE) reflects the number of calories needed when the body is at rest. Once you determine your BEE, you can factor in your activity level to estimate how many calories you burn each day.

Use the Harris-Benedict Equation (1919) below to find out how many calories you need to maintain your weight.

Fill in the blank boxes and compute.

> Conversions:
> weight in pounds ÷ 2.2 = weight in kilograms (kg)
> height in inches x 2.54 = height in centimeters (cm)

Females:
BEE = 655 + 9.6 x wt(Kg) + 1.8 x ht(cm) − 4.7 x age(years)
BEE = 655 + (9.6 x □□.□) + (1.8 x □□□) − 4.7 x □□
    = □□□□ Kcal/day

Males:
BEE = 66 + 13.7 x wt(Kg) + 5 x ht(cm) − 6.7 x age(years)
BEE = 66 + (13.7 x □□.□) + (5 x □□□) − 6.7 x □□
    = □□□□ Kcal/day

Adjustment in Body Weight for Overweight People:
If you weigh more than 125% of your ideal body weight use the following formula to determine your weight in pounds for the Harris-Benedict equation.

{[Actual body weight − Ideal body weight (IBW)] x 0.25} + IBW =

LIFE STYLE ACTIVITY FACTORS*

Activity Category		Activity Factor
Very Light (sedentary)	seated work minimal or no exercise	1.3–1.4
Light	mostly seated work irregular exercise	1.5
Moderate	seated and lightly active work some regular activity but little strenuous exercise	1.6–1.7
Extremely Active	strenuous work heavy exercise	1.8–2.2

* Adapted from Shetty P.S., et al., 1996 and FAO/WHO/UNO, 1985 and Food & Nutrition Board, National Research Council, NAS, 1989 and National Academy Press, 1989.

Identify your Life Style Activity Factor (see chart above) and multiply by your BEE to find your daily energy need. Most people fall between the light and moderate activity factors. Pray to find the right activity factor for you.

Total Energy Requirement = ☐☐☐☐ Kcals/day x ☐.☐ Activity Factor

Your Total Energy Requirement tells you how many calories you need for maintenance. To gain or lose weight, you must add or subtract calories from this maintenance level. To lose weight subtract the amounts below, and to gain, add the same amounts.

+/- 500 calories for 1lb/wk weight loss.

+/- 750 calories for 1½lb/wk weight loss.

+/- 1000 calories for 2lb/wk weight loss.

For weight loss: *Do not drop below 1000 calories/day.*

Before You Begin

Now that you have established your weight loss (or weight gain) goals, it is important to keep in mind that weight loss, gain, or maintenance cannot be achieved by diet alone. There are three components to forming and keeping healthy habits.

These are: 1. good nutrition
2. exercise
3. behavior modification

Through diet, discipline, and discipleship, 3D helps members work all three components into their life style.

Try to approach the 3D program as a better, healthier way to live your life, rather than "just another diet program." By doing so, you can minimize feelings of deprivation or urges to "cheat." By focusing on healthier habits, rather than on the bathroom scale, you are more likely to be successful in reaching your goals.

Let's Talk Nutrition

The USDA, as well as the American Institute for Cancer Research, promotes a low-fat, high-fiber diet. We know that by improving our weight status, avoiding fats, and eating a diet rich in vegetables, fruits, and whole grains, we can help reduce the risk of heart disease, diabetes, and cancer. As always, the 3D program is at the cutting edge of what we know about diet and disease. By using the exchange lists that follow, in combination with using food labels to monitor fat and fiber intake, we can easily achieve a low-fat, high-fiber meal plan.

The Exchange Lists

The Exchange Lists divide our basic food requirements into six categories: Milk, Vegetables, Fruit, Starch, Meat, and Fat. Foods are placed in the categories according to similar vitamin, mineral, carbohydrate, protein, and fat content. Each group provides its own particular type of nutrients, and we need a balance of all the groups for good nutrition. Within each category, the portion size for each exchange is important.

The Exchange Lists reflect the latest thinking in the area of nutrition, based on concern for total caloric intake and for modification of fat.

List 1: STARCH EXCHANGES include breads, cereals, grains, pasta, beans, peas and lentils, and starchy vegetables.

List 2: FRUIT EXCHANGES give the serving sizes for fruit and fruit juices.

List 3: MILK EXCHANGES include most dairy products.

List 4: VEGETABLE EXCHANGES include all vegetables except starchy vegetables.

List 5: MEAT EXCHANGES include not only meat, but also other protein-rich foods.

List 6: FAT EXCHANGES have been revised to show the differences in the kinds of fat.

The Exchanges

We have been talking about "Exchange Lists," and you may ask—"What exactly are they?" When we say "exchange," we mean "substitute." Within each food group, if you do not want one food, you may substitute another. But only substitute foods within a given group—i.e., green beans instead of tomatoes. (You cannot substitute green beans for orange juice.)

It is important to weigh and measure your food according to the amounts listed, as we are very much deceived by our own eyes. (It is amazing to measure a 2-inch apple and see how small it is!) This self-deception is especially noticeable in the Fat Exchange List. By habit, we use much more butter or margarine than we realize and need—one teaspoon of margarine for toast is not very much! Fats are also a source of many calories; for instance, a teaspoon of butter or margarine has twice as many calories as a teaspoon of sugar.

If you are already familiar with the Exchange Lists, the Meat Group will represent a change. As stated above, meats can contain many calories of fat, and they are one of the reasons for greater clarification in the meat group—for extra lean-, lean- and medium-fat meats. A high-fat meat list is not included because these meats should almost never be eaten. It would be easy to actually gain weight by eating too much high-fat meat. So remember, if you eat a medium- or high-fat meat, you need to count the extra grams of fat so that you can keep within your daily fat allowance.

You may have noticed that when we get older our caloric need decreases. Additional exercise does help, but you may well need help readjusting your eating habits from your teens and twenties.

As previously mentioned, we receive calories (energy) from the proteins, fats, and carbohydrates in foods—starches and sugar being the most common carbohydrates. Protein yields amino acids and nitrogen which are necessary for life, and fat provides a very concentrated source of calories. Vitamins and various minerals are present in all of the food groups, which is why we need a *balance of all the food groups* in our daily diet to have good health.

The 3D diet is not new, but our approach to dieting takes on a new slant when we ask Jesus to help us "exchange" some of our old eating habits for new ones.

Model Meal Plan

Use the following chart as a guideline for incorporating the exchanges into your daily routine. The exchanges are divided into small meals with snacks. Eating regularly will help prevent cycles of hunger and overeating as well as give your body the energy it needs throughout the day. If necessary, you may adapt this plan to your own life style. However, as you rearrange exchanges and meals, remember to keep meals balanced, and to not space meals too far apart.

Exchanges	Calories per day							
	1000	1200	1500	1800	2000	2400	2600	3000
Breakfast								
Meat			1	1	1	1	1	2
Bread	1	1	1	2	2	3	3	4
Fruit	1	1	1	1	1	1	2	2
Milk	1	1	1	1	1	1	1	1
Fat						1	2	2
Lunch								
Meat	2	3	3	3	3	4	4	4
Bread	1	2	2	2	3	3	3	3
Vegetable	2	2	2	2	2	2	2	2
Fruit				1	1	2	2	2
Milk								
Fat	1	1	1	1	1	2	2	2
Snack								
Meat								
Bread				1	1	2	2	3
Vegetable		1	1	1	1	1	2	2
Fruit	1	1	1	1	1	1	1	2
Milk	1	1	1	1	1	1	1	1
Dinner								
Meat	3	3	3	4	4	4	4	5
Bread	2	2	2	2	3	3	4	4
Vegetable	2	2	2	2	2	2	2	3
Fruit								1
Milk								
Fat		2	2	2	2	2	2	2
Snack								
Bread			1	1	1	1	1	1
Fruit			1	1	1	1	1	1
Milk					1	1	1	1

List 1 Starch Exchanges

Cereals, grains, pasta, breads, crackers, snacks, starchy vegetables, and cooked beans, peas, and lentils are starches. In general, one starch is:
- ½ cup of cereal, grain, pasta, or starchy vegetable,
- 1 ounce of a bread product, such as 1 slice of bread,
- ¾ to 1 ounce of most snack foods. (Some snack foods may also have added fat.)

One starch exchange equals:
- 15 grams carbohydrate,
- 3 grams protein,
- 0-1 grams fat, and
- 80 calories.

Bread

Bagel	½ (1 oz)
Bread, reduced-calorie	2 slices (1½ oz)
Bread, white, whole-wheat, pumpernickel, rye	1 slice (1 oz)
Bread sticks, crisp, 4 in. long x ½ in.	2 (⅔ oz)
English muffin	½
Hot dog or hamburger bun	½ (1 oz)
Pita, 6 in. across	½
Raisin bread, unfrosted	1 slice (1 oz)
Roll, plain, small	1 (1oz)
Tortilla, corn, 6 in. across	1
Tortilla, flour, 6 in. across	1
Waffle, 4½ in. square, reduced-fat	1

Cereals and Grains

Bran cereals	½ cup
Bulgur	½ cup
Cereals	½ cup
Cereals, unsweetened, ready-to-eat	¾ cup
Cornmeal (dry)	3 Tbsp.
Couscous	⅓ cup
Flour (dry)	3 Tbsp.
Granola, low-fat	¼ cup

Grape-Nuts® . . . . ¼ cup
Grits . . . . ½ cup
Kasha . . . . ½ cup
Millet . . . . ¼ cup
Muesli . . . . ¼ cup
Oats . . . . ½ cup
Pasta . . . . ½ cup
Puffed cereal . . . . .1½ cups
Rice milk . . . . ½ cup
Rice, white or brown . . . . ⅓ cup
Shredded Wheat® . . . . ½ cup
Sugar-frosted cereal . . . . ½ cup
Wheat germ . . . . .3 Tbsp

Starchy Vegetables

Baked beans . . . . ⅓ cup
Corn . . . . ½ cup
Corn on cob, medium . . . . .1 (5 oz)
Mixed vegetables with corn, peas, or pasta . . . . .1 cup
Peas, green . . . . ½ cup
Plantain . . . . ½ cup
Potato, baked or boiled . . . . .1 small (3 oz)
Potato, mashed . . . . ½ cup
Squash, winter (acorn, butternut) . . . . .1 cup
Yam, sweet potato, plain . . . . ½ cup

Crackers And Snacks

Animal crackers 8
Graham crackers, 2½ in. square 3
Matzoh . . . . ¾ oz
Melba toast . . . . .4 slices
Oyster crackers 24
Popcorn (popped, no fat added or low-fat microwave) . . .3 cups
Pretzels . . . . ¾ oz
Rice cakes, 4 in. across 2
Saltine-type crackers 6
Snack chips, fat-free (tortilla, potato) . . . . .15–20 (¾ oz)
Whole-wheat crackers, no fat added . . . . .2–5 (¾ oz)

Beans, Peas, And Lentils
(Count as 1 starch exchange, plus 1 very lean meat exchange.)
Beans and peas (garbanzo, pinto,
  kidney, white, split, black-eyed) . . . . .½ cup
Lima beans . . . . .⅔ cup
Lentils . . . . .½ cup
Miso* . . . . .3 Tbsp

* = 400 mg or more of sodium per exchange.

Starchy Foods, Prepared With Fat
(Count as 1 starch exchange, plus 1 fat exchange.)
Biscuit, 2½ in. across 1
Chow mein noodles . . . . .½ cup
Corn bread, 2 in. cube . . . . .1 (2 oz)
Crackers, round butter type 6
Croutons . . . . .1 cup
French-fried potatoes . . . . .16–25 (3 oz)
Granola . . . . .¼ cup
Muffin, small . . . . .1 (1½ oz)
Pancake, 4 in. across 2
Popcorn, microwave . . . . .3 cups
Sandwich crackers, cheese or peanut butter filling 3
Stuffing, bread (prepared) . . . . .⅓ cup
Taco shell, 6 in. across 2
Waffle, 4½ in. square 1
Whole-wheat crackers, fat added . . . . .4–6 (1 oz)

Starches often swell in cooking, so a small amount of uncooked starch will become a much larger amount of cooked food. The following table shows some of the changes.

Food (Starch Group)	Uncooked	Cooked
Oatmeal	3 Tbsp	½ cup
Cream of Wheat	2 Tbsp	½ cup
Grits	3 Tbsp	½ cup
Rice	2 Tbsp	⅓ cup
Spaghetti	¼ cup	½ cup
Noodles	⅓ cup	½ cup
Macaroni	¼ cup	½ cup
Dried beans	¼ cup	½ cup
Dried peas	¼ cup	½ cup
Lentils	3 Tbsp	½ cup

Common Measurements

3 tsp = 1 Tbsp
4 Tbsp = ¼ cup
5⅓ Tbsp = ⅓ cup
4 ounces = ½ cup
8 ounces = 1 cup
1 cup = ½ pint

List 2 Fruit Exchanges

Fresh, frozen, canned, and dried fruits and fruit juices are on this list. In general, one fruit exchange is:
- 1 small to medium fresh fruit,
- ½ cup of canned or fresh fruit or fruit juice,
- ¼ cup of dried fruit.

One fruit exchange equals:
- 15 grams carbohydrate and
- 60 calories.
- The weight includes skin, core, seeds, and rind.

Fruit

Apple, unpeeled, small	1 (4 oz)
Applesauce, unsweetened	½ cup
Apples, dried	4 rings
Apricots, fresh	4 whole (5½ oz)
Apricots, dried	8 halves
Apricots, canned	½ cup
Banana, small	1 (4 oz)
Blackberries	¾ cup
Blueberries	¾ cup
Cantaloupe, small	⅓ melon (11 oz) or 1 cup cubes
Cherries, sweet, fresh	12 (3 oz)
Cherries, sweet, canned	½ cup
Dates	3
Figs, fresh	1½ large or 2 medium (3½ oz)
Figs, dried	1½
Fruit cocktail	½ cup
Grapefruit, large	½ (11 oz)
Grapefruit sections, canned	¾ cup
Grapes, small	17 (3 oz)
Honeydew melon	1 slice (10 oz) or 1 cup cubes
Kiwi	1 (3½ oz)
Mandarin oranges, canned	¾ cup
Mango, small	½ fruit (5½ oz) or ½ cup

Nectarine, small . . . . .1 (5 oz)
Orange, small . . . . .1 (6½ oz)
Papaya . . . . .½ fruit (8 oz) or 1 cup cubes
Peach, medium, fresh . . . . .1 (6 oz)
Peaches, canned . . . . .½ cup
Pear, large, fresh . . . . .½ (4 oz)
Pears, canned . . . . .½ cup
Pineapple, fresh . . . . .¾ cup
Pineapple, canned . . . . .½ cup
Plums, small . . . . .2 (5 oz)
Plums, canned . . . . .½ cup
Prunes, dried 3
Raisins . . . . .2 Tbsp
Raspberries . . . . .1 cup
Strawberries . . . . .1¼ cup whole berries
Tangerines, small . . . . .2 (8 oz)
Watermelon . . . . .1 slice (13½ oz) or 1¼ cup cubes

Fruit Juice
Apple juice/cider . . . . .½ cup
Cranberry juice cocktail . . . . .⅓ cup
Cranberry juice cocktail, reduced-calorie . . . . .1 cup
Fruit juice blends, 100% juice . . . . .⅓ cup
Grape juice . . . . .⅓ cup
Grapefruit juice . . . . .½ cup
Orange juice . . . . .½ cup
Pineapple juice . . . . .½ cup
Prune juice . . . . .⅓ cup

One milk exchange equals:
- 12 grams carbohydrate and
- 8 grams protein.

Skim And Low-fat Milk
(0-3 grams fat per serving)

Skim milk . . . . .1 cup

½% milk . . . . .1 cup

1% milk . . . . .1 cup

Nonfat or low-fat buttermilk . . . . .1 cup

Evaporated skim milk . . . . .½ cup

Nonfat dry milk . . . . .⅓ cup dry

Plain nonfat yogurt . . . . .¾ cup

Nonfat or low-fat fruit-flavored yogurt sweetened
    with aspartame or with a non-nutritive sweetener . . . . .1 cup

Reduced-fat
(5 grams fat per serving)

2% milk . . . . .1 cup

Plain low-fat yogurt . . . . .¾ cup

Sweet acidophilus milk . . . . .1 cup

Whole Milk
(8 grams fat per serving)

Whole milk . . . . .1 cup

Evaporated whole milk . . . . .½ cup

Goat's milk . . . . .1 cup

Kefir . . . . .1 cup

List 4 Vegetable Exchanges

In general, one vegetable exchange is:
- ½ cup of cooked vegetables or vegetable juice,
- 1 cup of raw vegetables.

One vegetable exchange equals:
- 5 grams carbohydrate,
- 2 grams protein,
- 0 grams fat, and
- 25 calories.

Artichoke
Artichoke hearts
Asparagus
Beans (green, wax, Italian)
Bean sprouts
Beets
Broccoli
Brussels sprouts
Cabbage
Carrots
Cauliflower
Celery
Cucumber
Eggplant
Green onions or scallions
Greens (collard, kale,
    mustard, turnip)
Kohlrabi
Leeks
Mixed vegetables
    (without corn, peas, or pasta)

Mushrooms
Okra
Onions
Pea pods
Peppers (all varieties)
Radishes
Salad greens (endive, escarole,
    lettuce, romaine, spinach)
Sauerkraut*
Spinach
Summer squash
Tomato
Tomatoes, canned
Tomato sauce*
Tomato/vegetable juice*
Turnips
Water chestnuts
Watercress
Zucchini

* = 400 mg or more sodium per exchange

List 5 Meat Exchanges

In general, one meat exchange is:
- 1 oz meat, fish, poultry, or cheese,
- ½ cup beans, peas, or lentils.

Very Lean Meat And Substitutes List
One exchange equals:
- 0 grams carbohydrate,
- 7 grams protein,
- 0-1 grams fat, and
- 35 calories.

One very lean meat exchange is equal to any one of the following items.

Poultry: Chicken or turkey (white meat, no skin),
Cornish hen (no skin) . . . . .1 oz

Fish: Fresh or frozen cod, flounder, haddock, halibut,
trout; tuna fresh or canned in water . . . . .1 oz

Shellfish: Clams, crab, lobster, scallops, shrimp,
imitation shellfish . . . . .1 oz

Game: Duck or pheasant (no skin), venison,
buffalo, ostrich . . . . .1 oz

Cheese with 1 gram or less fat per ounce:
Nonfat or low-fat cottage cheese . . . . .¼ cup
Fat-free cheese . . . . .1 oz

Other: Processed sandwich meats with 1 gram or less
fat per ounce, such as deli thin, shaved meats,
chipped beef*, turkey ham . . . . .1 oz
Egg whites 2
Egg substitutes, plain . . . . .¼ cup
Hot dogs with 1 gram or less fat per ounce* . . . . .1 oz
Kidney (high in cholesterol) . . . . .1 oz
Sausage with 1 gram or less fat per ounce . . . . .1 oz

Count as one very lean meat and one starch exchange.
Beans, peas, lentils (cooked) . . . . .½ cup

* = 400 mg or more sodium per exchange.

Lean Meat And Substitutes List

One exchange equals:
- 0 grams carbohydrate,
- 7 grams protein,
- 3 grams fat, and
- 55 calories.

One lean meat exchange is equal to any one of the following items.

Beef: USDA Select or Choice grades of lean beef
trimmed of fat, such as round, sirloin, and flank
steak; tenderloin; roast (rib, chuck, rump);
steak (T-bone, porterhouse, cubed), ground round . . . . .1 oz
Pork: Lean pork, such as fresh ham; canned, cured,
or boiled ham; Canadian bacon*; tenderloin, center
loin chop . . . . .1 oz
Lamb: Roast, chop, leg . . . . .1 oz
Veal: Lean chop, roast . . . . .1 oz
Poultry: Chicken, turkey (dark meat, no skin),
chicken (white meat, with skin), domestic
duck or goose (well-drained of fat, no skin) . . . . .1 oz
Fish: Herring (uncreamed or smoked) . . . . .1 oz
Oysters . . . . .6 medium
Salmon (fresh or canned), catfish . . . . .1 oz
Sardines (canned) . . . . .2 medium
Tuna (canned in oil, drained) . . . . .1 oz
Game: Goose (no skin), rabbit . . . . .1 oz
Cheese: 4.5%-fat cottage cheese .¼ cup
Grated Parmesan . . . . .2 Tbsp
Cheese with 3 grams or less fat per ounce . . . . .1 oz
Other:
Hot dogs with 3 grams or less fat per ounce* . . . . .1½ oz
Processed sandwich meat with 3 grams or less
fat per ounce, such as turkey pastrami or kielbasa . . . . .1 oz
Liver, heart (high in cholesterol) .1 oz

* = 400 mg or more sodium per exchange.

Medium-Fat Meat And Substitutes List

One exchange equals:
- 0 grams carbohydrate,
- 7 grams protein,
- 5 grams fat, and
- 75 calories.

One medium-fat meat exchange is equal to any one of the following items.

Beef: Most beef products fall into this category (ground beef, meatloaf, corned beef, short ribs, prime grades of meat trimmed of fat, such as prime rib) ....1 oz

Pork: Top loin, chop, Boston butt, cutlet ....1 oz

Lamb: Rib roast, ground ....1 oz

Veal: Cutlet (ground or cubed, unbreaded) ....1 oz

Poultry: Chicken (dark meat, with skin), ground turkey or ground chicken, fried chicken (with skin) ....1 oz

Fish: Any fried fish product ....1 oz

Cheese: With 5 grams or less fat per ounce

    Feta ....1 oz

    Mozzarella ....1 oz

    Ricotta ....¼ cup (2 oz)

Other:

    Egg (high in cholesterol, limit to 3 per week) 1

    Sausage with 5 grams or less fat per ounce ....1 oz

    Soy milk ....1 cup

    Tempeh ....¼ cup

    Tofu ....4 oz or ½ cup

List 6 Fat Exchanges

Fats are divided into three groups, based on the main type of fat they contain: monounsaturated, polyunsaturated, and saturated. Saturated fats are linked with heart disease and cancer, and saturated fats have been associated with an *increase* in blood cholesterol (a possible risk factor in coronary heart disease). A physician may advise a reduction of foods high in this kind of fat. If you are going to add fats, it's best to pick fats from the monounsaturated fats list. In general, one fat exchange is:

- 1 teaspoon of regular margarine or vegetable oil, or
- 1 tablespoon of regular salad dressings.

Monounsaturated Fats List
One fat exchange equals 5 grams fat and 45 calories.

Avocado, medium	⅛ (1 oz)
Oil (canola, olive, peanut)	1 tsp
Olives: ripe (black)	8 large
green, stuffed*	10 large
Nuts: almonds, cashews	6 nuts
mixed (50% peanuts)	6 nuts
peanuts	10 nuts
pecans	4 halves
Peanut butter, smooth or crunchy	2 tsp
Sesame seeds	1 Tbsp
Tahini paste	2 tsp

Polyunsaturated Fats List
One fat exchange equals 5 grams fat and 45 calories.

Margarine: stick, tub, or squeeze	1 tsp
lower-fat (30% to 50% vegetable oil)	1 Tbsp
Mayonnaise: regular	1 tsp
reduced-fat	1 Tbsp
Nuts, walnuts, English	4 halves
Oil (corn, safflower, soybean)	1 tsp
Salad dressing: regular*	1 Tbsp
reduced-fat	2 Tbsp

* = 400 mg or more sodium per exchange.

Miracle Whip Salad Dressing®: regular . . . . .2 tsp
    reduced-fat . . . . .1 Tbsp
Seeds: pumpkin, sunflower . . . . .1 Tbsp

* = 400 mg or more sodium per exchange

Saturated Fats List **
One fat exchange equals 5 grams of fat and 45 calories.

Bacon, cooked . . . . .1 slice (20 slices/lb)
Bacon, grease . . . . .1 tsp
Butter: stick . . . . .1 tsp
    whipped . . . . .2 tsp
    reduced-fat . . . . .1 Tbsp
Chitterlings, boiled . . . . .1 Tbsp (½ oz)
Coconut, sweetened, shredded .2 Tbsp
Cream, half and half . . . . .2 Tbsp
Cream cheese: regular . . . . .1 Tbsp (½ oz)
    reduced-fat . . . . .2 Tbsp (1 oz)
Fatback or salt pork, see below†
Shortening or lard . . . . .1 tsp
Sour cream: regular . . . . .2 Tbsp
    reduced-fat . . . . .3 Tbsp

† Use a piece 1 in. x 1 in. x ¼ in. if you plan to eat the fatback cooked with vegetables. Use a piece 2 in. x 1 in. x ½ in. when eating only the vegetables with the fatback removed.

** Saturated fats can raise blood cholesterol levels.

Foods with a serving size listed should be limited to three servings per day maximum. Many fat-free foods are high in sugar and may have trace amounts of fats which can add extra calories.

Fat-free Or Reduced-fat Foods

Cream cheese, fat-free . . . . .1 Tbsp
Creamers, nondairy, liquid . . . . .1 Tbsp
Creamers, nondairy, powdered .2 tsp
Mayonnaise, fat-free . . . . .1 Tbsp
Mayonnaise, reduced-fat . . . . .1 tsp
Margarine, fat-free . . . . .4 Tbsp
Margarine, reduced-fat . . . . .1 tsp
Miracle Whip®, non-fat . . . . .1 Tbsp
Miracle Whip®, reduced-fat . . . . .1 tsp
Nonstick cooking spray
Salad dressing, fat-free . . . . .1 Tbsp
Salad dressing, fat-free, Italian .1 Tbsp
Salsa . . . . .¼ cup
Sour cream, fat-free, reduced-fat . . . . .1 Tbsp
Whipped topping, regular or light . . . . 2 Tbsp

Sugar-free Or Low-sugar Foods

Candy, hard, sugar-free . . . . .1 candy
Gelatin dessert, sugar-free
Gelatin, unflavored
Gum, sugar-free
Jam or jelly, low-sugar or light . . . . 2 tsp
Sugar substitutes†
Syrup, sugar-free . . . . .2 Tbsp

Sugar substitutes, alternatives, or replacements that are approved by the Food and Drug Administration (FDA) are safe to use. Common brand names include:

Equal® (aspartame)   Sweet-10® (saccharin)
Sprinkle Sweet® (saccharin)   Sugar Twin® (saccharin)
Sweet One® (acesulfame K)   Sweet 'n Low® (saccharin)

Drinks

Bouillon, broth, consommé *
Bouillon or broth, low-sodium
Carbonated or mineral water
Club soda
Cocoa powder, unsweetened . . . . .1 Tbsp
Coffee
Diet soft drinks, sugar-free
Drink mixes, sugar-free
Tea
Tonic water, sugar-free

Condiments

Catsup . . . . .1 Tbsp
Horseradish
Lemon juice
Lime juice
Mustard
Pickles, dill * . . . . .1½ large
Soy sauce, regular or light *
Taco sauce . . . . .1 Tbsp
Vinegar

Seasonings

Be careful with seasonings that contain sodium or are salts, such as garlic or celery salt, and lemon pepper.

Flavoring extracts
Garlic
Herbs, fresh or dried
Pimento
Spices
Tabasco® or hot pepper sauce
Wine, used in cooking
Worcestershire sauce

* = 400 mg or more of sodium per exchange.

How much fat?

The latest recommendation from the American Institute for Cancer Research recommends that total fat intake should be between 15% to no more than 30% of a person's total daily calories. This is in keeping with the American Heart Association's Guidelines to help reduce high cholesterol and heart disease.

Below is a fat budget plan showing you different fat gram amounts for different calorie levels. One is worked out for 25% fat calories, the second for 20%, and the third for 15%. Now here is the really hard part: you should not go any lower than the lowest figure on this chart for your daily calorie allowance. Fat is essential in your diet to maintain normal metabolism—too little fat is not good. After looking over the chart, pray and decide what you should do for the next 12 weeks—and fill in the sentence at the bottom of the page with your commitment.

If you follow the meal plans (see pg. 51) and choose primarily non-fat dairy products and extra lean or lean meats from the exchange lists, you will easily be within the recommended range. You may want to take the time to actually add up the fat grams you ate for a few days so you can double check that you are meeting your fat gram goals.

Fat Budget Plan

Daily Caloric Allowance	1000	1200	1500	1850	2000	2400
25% Fat Calories (Daily calories x .25)	250	300	375	463	500	600
# Fat Grams allowed (Fat calories ÷ 9)	28	33	41	51	55	67

Daily Caloric Allowance	1000	1200	1500	1850	2000	2400
20% Fat Calories (Daily calories x .2)	200	240	300	370	400	480
# Fat Grams allowed (Fat calories ÷ 9)	22	26	33	41	44	53

Daily Caloric Allowance	1000	1200	1500	1850	2000	2400
15% Fat Calories (Daily calories x .15)	150	180	225	278	300	360
# Fat Grams allowed (Fat calories ÷ 9)	17	20	25	31	33	40

My Personal Fat Budget should be _____ grams of fat for the first 12 weeks of 3D. It is _____ % of _____ calories daily.

Let's Not Forget the Fiber

Most experts recommend that people eat between 20 and 30 grams of fiber daily. Most of us eat less than 12 grams. Some simple ways to boost your fiber intake are:

1. Choose *whole-grain* bread and bread products.
2. Start your day with a high-fiber cereal.
3. Instead of white rice or pasta, try wild rice or whole wheat couscous for an exciting new side dish.
4. Add a serving of beans or lentils to your usual menu.
5. Keep a supply of cut-up fruits and vegetables handy for snacking.

Look at the list below to get an idea of high-fiber foods.

High-Fiber Foods

Grains	Grams Fiber
Popcorn (3 c)	2.7
Bread (1 sl)	
Whole Wheat	1.6
White	0.5
Rice (1 c)	
Brown	3.3
White	1.0
Bulgur (1 c)	7.8
Barley (1 c)	6.5
Couscous (1 c)	21
Whole Wheat	
Couscous (1 c cooked)	7

Cereals (1 oz)	Grams Fiber*
Fiber One (½ c)	14.0
All Bran (½ c)	10.0
Bran Flakes (¾ c)	5.0
Multi Bran Chex (¾ c)	4.0
Wheat Chex (¾ c)	5.0
Quaker Corn Bran (¾ c)	5.0
Raisin Bran (½ c)	
Post	4.5
Kellogg's	3.5
Fruit and Fibre (½ c)	4.0
Oat Bran	
Cooked (⅔ c)	5.0
Shredded Wheat (1)	3.0

	Grams Fiber
Total (¾ c)	2.5
Wheaties (1 c)	3.0
Wheat Germ (3 tbsp)	3.3
Oatmeal, cooked	
Regular (½ c)	4.0
Multi-Grain (½ c)	5.0
Grape-Nuts (1/4 c)	2.5

Fruits	Grams Fiber
Apple (with skin)	2.8
Banana	3.0
Blueberries (½ c)	1.5
Orange	2.6
Pear (with skin)	4.0
Prunes (3)	1.6
Strawberries (1 c)	3.9

Crackers (½ oz)	Grams Fiber*
Wasa Crispbread	
Fiber Plus (1½)	4.3
Sesame Rye (1½)	3.6
Ryvita Crispbread	
High Fiber (1½)	2.5
Kavli Crispbread	
Thick (1½)	3.0
Ry-Krisp Natural or	
Seasoned (2 triples)	3.0

* See next page.

Legumes (½ cup cooked)	Grams Fiber	Starchy Vegetables (1/2 cup cooked)	Grams Fiber
Black Beans	6.5	Peas	3.0
Kidney Beans	5.0	Corn	3.4
Pinto Beans	5.9	Potato, baked	1.6
Chick-peas	4.4	Squash, summer	1.5
Lentils	7.8	Squash, winter	3.0
Lima Beans	4.0	Yams	3.8

Vegetables (1 cup raw)	Grams Fiber
Broccoli	2.2
Cabbage	1.5
Carrots	4.6
Green Beans	3.5
Lettuce	0.5
Spinach	1.5
Tomatoes	2.4
Asparagus	2.5

* Based on product information—check labels for product information changes. All other fiber values from Nutrition Data System Version 24. University of Minnesota, 1993, or:

U.S. Department of Agriculture, Agricultural Research Service. 1997. USDA Nutrient Database for Standard Reference, Release 11-1. Nutrient Data Laboratory Home Page, http://www.nal.usda.gov/fnic/foodcomp

All registered trademarks are acknowledged.

Nutritional Notes

PROTEINS are the body's building blocks; you need them for muscle and connective tissue growth. They do not stimulate your body's insulin production, and that means your blood sugar doesn't drop and you don't feel as hungry later on. Proteins also take a little while to digest, so they make you feel fuller longer. Too much protein or any one nutrient is not good for your body. Avoid diets that are extreme in any one nutrient. Think balance!

CARBOHYDRATES supply vital nutritional needs in our diet and are our primary source of fuel. Carbohydrates can be found in many food sources including milk, grains, fruits, and vegetables. Items like sugar, honey, molasses, and corn syrup are primarily pure carbohydrates and are often called simple sugars because of their molecular structure. Unlike protein, when you ingest carbohydrates, your blood sugar rises. Food made from simple carbohydrates like candy bars, cookies, and soft drinks, can cause a rapid rise in your blood sugar level. This rapid rise can cause a stimulatory effect, which is often why people turn to sweets for a "pick-up" or energy boost. After the rapid rise, a fall in blood sugar usually occurs and the person may crave more sweets. This is how a cycle of eating too many sweets and overeating begins.

Some people are more carbohydrate sensitive than others. If you know you have difficulty handling your sweet intake, it's best to always avoid dessert food. It is also important that your total daily carbohydrate is not in excess. Remember to keep your meals balanced and to eat regular snacks. These strategies, which form part of the 3D program, will help minimize cravings for sweets and will help you stay energetic throughout the day.

FATS increase the viscosity (stickiness) of blood, and sticky blood clumps together and attaches to the walls of blood vessels, interfering with blood flow and cell breathing. A lot is being written about the danger of high-fat diets. They can increase your risk of a stroke or heart attack and have also been implicated in certain cancers, particularly of the bowel and breast. You will ingest fat in many of the foods you eat normally, so it is best to avoid increasing your fat intake if at all possible. Triglycerides are fats normally present in the blood which are made from food. Being overweight or consuming too much fat, alcohol, and sugar may increase the blood triglycerides to an unacceptably high level.

CHOLESTEROL is a fatty substance produced by our bodies that is an essential part of every cell. Cholesterol is also found in foods of animal origin—eggs, milk, meat, fish, and poultry. Too much dietary cholesterol is unnecessary and may be harmful.

Too much cholesterol is harmful because saturated fat and dietary cholesterol (cholesterol in your food) are contributors to increased levels of total blood cholesterol in your body. Increased levels of total blood cholesterol have been identified as a risk factor for atherosclerosis—a build-up of fatty deposits on the inner walls of the blood vessels. Atherosclerosis is a leading risk factor for heart disease and stroke.

There are different kinds of cholesterol. Cholesterol is one blood reading that has several parts. The LDL-Cholesterol (low-density lipoprotein) and the HDL-Cholesterol (high-density lipoprotein) make up your blood cholesterol. The LDL-Cholesterol is the most harmful.

LDL is commonly known as the "bad" cholesterol because it deposits artery-clogging cholesterol on the walls of the blood vessels. HDL, on the other hand, is called the "good" cholesterol, because it sweeps cholesterol out of the body.

Cholesterol is measured by a simple blood test that shows milligrams of total cholesterol (HDL and LDL) per deciliter of blood. Total cholesterol over 185 mg/dl for children or 240mg/dl for adults is undesirably high.

The American Heart Association recommends that healthy adults eat no more than 300mg of dietary cholesterol per day. By eating fewer animal products and saturated fats, and eating more fruits, vegetables, fish, and whole grains, you can reduce your dietary cholesterol. Choose polyunsaturated and monounsaturated fat rather than saturated fat.

(National Institute of Health)

The 8 best cooking oils have the least saturated fat and no cholesterol:

Canola	Peanut
Safflower	Olive
Sunflower	Soybean
Corn	Rice Bran

The 6 fats to avoid—although they are cholesterol-free, their high saturated fat levels will raise blood cholesterol:

Vegetable Shortening	Animal Fat Shortening
Cottonseed Oil	Palm Oil
Lard	Coconut

All of these fats need to be considered in your FAT exchanges. Even though the label says "No Cholesterol," they are all 100 percent fat—45 calories per teaspoon.

FIBER—An indigestible part of certain foods. Fiber is important in the diet as roughage, or bulk. Fiber is found in foods from the starch/bread, vegetable, and fruit exchange lists.

SOLUBLE FIBER has high water-holding capability and turns to gel during digestion. This process slows digestion and the rate of nutrient absorption from the stomach and intestine. Soluable fiber is found in oat bran, pectins (from fruits and vegetables), and various "gums" which are found in nuts, seeds, and legumes such as beans, lentils, and peas. This type of fiber may play a role in smoothing out the glycemic response of foods, and in reducing the likelihood of atherosclerosis.

INSOLUBLE FIBER is found in foods such as wheat bran and other whole grains, and has poor water-holding capability. It appears to speed the passage of foods through the stomach and intestines, and increases fecal bulk. This type of fiber probably does not affect glycemia response or atherosclerosis.

USE LESS SALT—Most of us eat too much salt. The sodium in salt can cause the body to retain water, and in some people it may raise blood pressure. High blood pressure is made worse by eating too much salt and sodium. So try to use less salt in cooking and at the table. Decrease the amount of high-sodium foods such as ham, bacon, salted crackers, pickles, olives, and canned soups.

Hints

As you proceed through the twelve-week 3D session, you might crave some special favorite foods—particularly at holiday times. Try to fit these foods and their ingredients into the Exchange Lists and still remain on the diet. The *Heart Smart Cookbook* distributed by 3D is a 263-page cookbook published by the Henry Ford Heart and Vascular Institute. The recipes are not only outstanding, but also provide complete nutritional information, including food exchanges and fats. (See coupon in back of this manual.)

Read labels. Low-calorie, reduced calorie or lite does not mean calorie-free. This is especially true of "low-calorie" salad dressings, some of which contain up to 40 or 50 calories per tablespoon. We advise using only those that have fewer than ten calories per tablespoon. The word "dietetic" can be misleading; it, too, does not mean calorie-free, and even products labeled "dietetic" should not be eaten in large amounts—an overall balance is healthy.

Keep non-fat dry milk and skimmed evaporated milk on hand. These are easy to cook with and have fewer calories than modified skimmed milk.

Buy natural fruit juices. Imitation fruit juices contain very little fruit juice and do contain much sugar and many calories.

Learn about spices and condiments; many add flavor but not calories. You can use herbs and spices, rather than butter, to season vegetables. Spices can be used in sauces and salad dressings, in soups, stews, and meat loaf, and in fish, beef and poultry dishes. Dry mustard, garlic powder and garlic salt, onion powder and onion salt, celery seed and salt, curry powder, paprika, and dill seed are some of the spices and herbs that can be used in daily cooking. Did you know that paprika has more Vitamin C than any of the citrus fruits? Be bold in experimenting, using very small amounts to "test the taste," and you will soon discover your own favorites.

For a taste treat, try adding a bit of cinnamon, allspice, nutmeg, ginger, mace, or cloves to quick breads or muffins or coffee cakes, or to custards and creams, or add to root vegetables or the fall squashes for a different, delightful flavor.

The difference between salad and steamed vegetables is that steaming ruptures the starch molecule and makes for more satisfying food than just the bulk and fiber of salad. If the vegetables are steamed lightly, they will retain the filling quality of fiber and still unlock the starch.

When it is is difficult to weigh food there is a way to "eyeball" amounts. One ounce of meat is the size of a small matchbox, 3 ounces of meat is the size of a deck of cards, and 8 ounces of meat is the size of a small paperback book.

In restaurants you can substitute fruit for the normal first courses.

Drink eight glasses of water daily.

Vegetarian Diet

We frequently receive inquiries regarding a Vegetarian Diet Plan. To meet that request, we have included an explanation of the Vegetarian Diet and a Model Diet Pattern Chart indicating calories and exchanges.

Pure vegetarians do not eat any foods of any animal origin for health reasons. Vegetarianism is gaining in popularity as many find that even occasional vegetarian meals help in lowering both food costs and fat consumption, and contribute fiber to the diet.

Lacto-ovo vegetarians who use eggs and dairy products as well as a variety of peas, beans, lentils, seeds, and nuts have no difficulty getting enough protein.

Vegans, who eliminate all animal products from their menus, must plan their meals more carefully. They will need serving sizes large enough to meet protein needs because plant proteins are less digestible than animal proteins. Vegans also need to plan their meals around complementary protein combinations. Because a vegan meal is bulky and low in protein digestibility, infants and young children will have difficulty eating enough of the plant protein choices to meet their recommended daily intakes for protein and iron. Vegans choose this diet primarily for philosophical reasons rather than health reasons.

In recent years, our affluent society has allowed most Americans to include meat in their diet. Lately, with the rising cost of meat and the latest medical findings which indicate a need to decrease dietary cholesterol and fats, many Americans are trying to cut down on their meat intake. The U.S. Recommended Dietary Allowance for protein has been *decreased* from 70 to 56 grams per day for men and from 55 to 46 grams for women, indicating that we do not need as much meat as we have been used to in the past.

How then do you plan a meatless diet and still eat the necessary protein and vitamins? While we may not need as much protein as we thought, we *do* need high-quality protein—that is, protein which has the essential amino acids. Proteins are the basis for all living tissue. There is no living tissue that does not contain some protein. The animal eats protein, whether it be animal or vegetable, breaks it down into amino acids by digestion, absorbs the amino acids, and from them forms its own protein. Therefore the amino acids are the units or the building stones from which the complex structure, protein, is built.

Experiments have been done which indicate that some amino acids are far more valuable than others. Animal proteins are, in general, well balanced in their amino acid distribution, whereas the protein in vegetables often is not complete in itself. When you learn how to *combine the various vegetables* you can form complete protein containing the proper amino acids. Although it is not our intent to give a complete course on combining foods, we do want to communicate how simple it is to combine the various vegetable proteins to obtain a complete protein such as is found in meat.

To achieve the right balance of vegetable proteins, it is important to choose a variety of fruits and vegetables. The dark green, leafy vegetables such as collards, kale, spinach, turnip and mustard greens, supply calcium and riboflavin; cabbage and broccoli also contain some calcium. Dried fruits, whole grains, and green leafy vegetables are also good sources of iron. Legumes, nuts and other seeds are good sources of the B-vitamins, along with germ and bran cereal grains. When a plant, or a portion of a plant, is rich in vitamins, it is also rich in minerals. So there is a variety of vitamins and minerals in fruits, green leafy vegetables, whole grains, legumes and other seeds and nuts.

The cereal grains comprise another important group, especially in their unrefined form. It has been found that the protein in the whole

43

grain is a superior product in quality and quantity, and the best protein is found in the germ and the bran. Whole-grain cereals and bread provide a moderate amount of protein, B-vitamins and minerals, but it is when the cereal grains are *combined* in a meal with legumes, such as peas and beans, that a complete protein is formed.

Legumes are a large group of plants of the pea family, having pods containing seeds. They have a higher protein content than any other vegetable family and they also enrich the soil with nitrogen.

In summary, here are some suggested combinations for complementary protein menu ideas:

1. Rice and beans
2. Wheat-soy bread
3. Baked beans and whole wheat bread
4. Pea soup and corn bread
5. Corn tortillas and beans
6. Whole wheat bread and milk or cheese
7. Pasta with milk or cheese
8. Rice and milk pudding

Complementary Plant Protein Sources

Food	Complementary Protein
Grains	Rice + legumes
	Corn + legumes
	Wheat + legumes
	Wheat + peanuts + milk
	Wheat + sesame + soybeans
	Rice + sesame
	Rice + brewer's yeast
Legumes	Legumes + rice
	Beans + wheat
	Beans + corn
	Soybeans + rice + wheat
	Soybeans + corn + milk
	Soybeans + peanuts + sesame
	Soybeans + peanuts + wheat + rice
Nuts and Seeds	Peanuts + sesame + soybeans
	Sesame + beans
	Sesame + soybeans + wheat
	Peanuts + sunflower seeds

Now that you have a better understanding of the vegetarian diet, how can you apply this in your 3D dietary program? The following chart illustrates the exchange list meal pattern for a vegetarian diet:

		1200 Calories	1500 Calories	1800 Calories
List 1	Starch	6	8	9
List 2	Fruit	3	3	5
List 3	Milk	1 cup low-fat	2 cups	2 cups
List 4	Vegetables	4	5	5
List 5	Meat	4	5	5
List 6	Fat	4	5	6

Vegetarian Diet Pattern Chart

EXCHANGES	CALORIES PER DAY		
	1200	1500	1800
	NUMBER OF EXCHANGES		
BREAKFAST			
Meat	1	1	1
Bread	1	1	2
Fruit	1	1	1
Milk	½	1	1
Fat	1	1	2
LUNCH			
Meat	2	2	2
Bread	2	3	3
Vegetable	2	2	2
Fruit	1	1	2
Milk	½	½	½
Fat	1	1	2
DINNER			
Meat	2	2	2
Bread	3	4	4
Vegetable	2	3	3
Fruit	1	1	2
Milk	—	½	½
Fat	1	2	2

These are some non-meat protein exchanges:

Lean Meat:

Dried beans and peas	½ c. = 1 protein and 1 bread
Low-fat cheese	1 oz. = 1 protein
Low-fat cottage cheese	¼ c. = 1 protein
Tofu, lowfat	4 oz. (2½" x 2¾" x 1") = 1 protein

Medium Fat—omit ½ fat:

Cheese—Mozzarella	1 oz. = 1 protein
Ricotta	1 oz. = 1 protein
Farmer's	1 oz. = 1 protein
Neufchatel	1 oz. = 1 protein
Parmesan	1 oz. = 1 protein
Egg (whole)	1 protein

If you have seen the word *tofu* and wondered what it is, this is a kind of soy cheese made for years in the Orient from soy flour and soy flakes. This cheese-like product is found in the fresh vegetable section of the grocery store. This protein product may be sliced, cubed, cut into chunks, ground, grated, or molded into shapes, and added to casseroles. It doesn't have much flavor in itself, but it takes on the flavor of the foods that it is mixed with.

Not only is the Vegetarian Diet economical, but has some other clear merits. Vegetarians increase their intake of complex carbohydrates, and through avoiding meat they decrease their intake of saturated fat. All these factors are a plus according to current dietary reports.

Food Allergy Problems

Studies have shown that eating one food repeatedly can cause our bodies to build up a sensitivity to that food and produce harmful effects. If you have eating habits that lean heavily on the same food meal after meal, you might want to try rotating your food over a four day period to see if you are overloading your body's defense system. If this is happening, your white blood corpuscles are responding to the "overload" as if they were being invaded by alien microbes and you may be unduly exhausted, or suffer from frequent headaches, sinus attacks, etc. Rotating foods could relieve the body of this artificially induced strain and permit it to function more effectively.

There are two basic ways to detect the foods to which you might be acutely sensitive, and the first is a natural outgrowth of rotating our foods. It involves limiting the intake of any one food to one meal out of 12. For instance, if you ate eggs for breakfast on Monday morning, you would not eat eggs again until Friday. Rotation makes it much easier to isolate those foods which are having adverse physical and mental effects on us.

The second way to uncover hidden food allergies is to systematically eliminate one suspect food at a time from our rotation and then re-introduce it and monitor our body and emotions for any aberrant effects. This is an old but well proven method of discovering allergies that doctors have been successfully using for generations.

Vitamins and Minerals

Vitamins and minerals are essential for human life. They serve a variety of functions and play a crucial role in many body processes. The first vitamin was discovered at the beginning of the twentieth century. When chemists discovered how to synthesize vitamins in the 1930s, deficiency-related diseases were almost eradicated by food fortification. Since then, many discoveries have been made about how vitamins and minerals contribute to optimum health. As science has progressed, so has the market for vitamin and mineral supplements. Today, many of us are overwhelmed with information about how much of a vitamin or mineral we should have, whether or not we should take supplements, and if so what is the form best absorbed by the body. There are many questions for which scientists unfortunately still do not have answers.

It is important to realize that if we eat a well balanced diet, most of us will get all the nutrients we need. There are some vitamins that may offer health benefits when taken in amounts higher than the recommended daily allowances. If you decide to supplement, make sure you have adequate information regarding the nutrient you are taking. Some vitamins and minerals are toxic at high levels and some may interfere with the effectiveness of certain medications. We suggest that you let your doctor be aware of any supplements you are taking. If you have questions regarding supplementation, try speaking to a registered dietitian or to a health professional.

Plateaus

A plateau is the point in your diet when you stop losing weight, even though you've been faithful to your diet plan. Every diet program includes setbacks and plateaus. You need to keep moving on, knowing that the program will work, even in the times you don't see the results. Dieters frequently get discouraged when they hit plateaus. Regardless of your faithfulness to your diet, these are to be expected.

The longer the calorie reduction lasts, the more the basal metabolic rate (rate of burning energy) slows down. Your body guards the fat, records a set-point weight, and will fight to defend that set point. As soon as your body gets over the shock of the initial water loss, it begins its fight back. It fights by lowering your basal metabolic rate so that you don't burn as much fat. Reducing your caloric intake further is not the answer. Exercise, of course, helps, but faithfulness and perseverance is necessary at these times! It helps to expect these temporary lulls—they are just part of the dieting process.

Be certain to talk about any discouragement so you won't "give up."

Anorexia Nervosa

More and more we are hearing about eating disorders which include anorexia nervosa and bulimia. The 3D program can be a help to people with these problems. Many reasons behind these problems are the same as those behind over-eating—"not feeling very good about who we are, constantly trying to prove our worth, over and over again, not only to parents and peers, but, most of all, to ourselves. And no matter what we achieved, it was never enough." (Quoted from *Deadly Diet*.)

To an anorexic, being or becoming overweight is the worst thing that can happen. Fat is disgusting and repulsive, and to be fat is to be a failure. Many have painful memories of teasing and rejection as children. Being in control of their food gives anorexics a feeling of safety.

The rigid need to be perfect drives the anorexic or bulimic ruthlessly. If any goal is reached, the next goal must be higher . . . and higher. Such a person is always striving!

There is help for anorexics and bulimics if they want help. The support of a caring, sharing 3D group can be an incredible blessing. Who better than a struggling dieter (who is herself just finding new healing in the area of food) can understand another's inner agony in the area of food?

Here are a few suggestions that we believe could be helpful:

- Eat three meals a day—do not skip a meal.
- Try to eat two snacks a day also.
- Do not weigh yourself except every other week.
- Keep your food sheet honestly. If you are in a group, be sure to give your sheet to the leaders for their support and encouragement.

It is very important that you talk about your feelings. This is a terrific way to use your Spiritual Journal. How do you feel when your weight goes up? Do you feel guilty when you eat? Remember, absolutely nothing is impossible with the Lord. In fact, he specializes in impossible things. Please keep in touch with us.

We recommend a book entitled *Deadly Diet*, which the American Anorexia/Bulimia Association has called "by far the most detailed and conscientiously recorded account of recovery . . . impressive and moving." It is a testimony of two women who learned how to face themselves and were healed. Copies are available from the 3D office.

Tips for Behavior Change

Try some of the following tips to help you control your food intake.

1. Rearrange food storage areas. Keep other family members' high fat/high sugar food in opaque containers (out of sight, out of mind).

2. Give away or throw away high fat/high sugar food gifts.

3. Keep healthy snacks available at work.

4. Don't eat in front of the TV set.

5. Do something enjoyable to distract yourself from eating (read a book or magazine, take a bubble bath, call a friend, find a hobby).

6. Prepare ahead. Plan and shop for meals in advance.

7. Use smaller plates and serving bowls.

8. Wait a half hour until the hunger or craving passes. Eat when you are truly hungry, not bored or stressed.

9. Choose restaurants with low-fat choices or flexible menus.

10. Reward yourself with little gifts (non-food items) for positive behavior.

Twenty-One Days of Simple, Easy-to-Plan, Low Fat Meals

DAY 1

Breakfast: 1/2 grapefruit
1 oz rice or oat cereal with skim milk
1/2 cup nonfat yogurt

Lunch: French Market Soup
Roll

Dinner: Tomato juice
Stir fry chicken with snow peas
1/2 c rice
wedge of lettuce with low fat dressing

DAY 2

Breakfast: 2 slices whole wheat toast with sugar free jam
1 orange
1/2 c no fat cottage cheese

Lunch: Chefs salad with 2 oz cheese
Non-fat salad dressing
3 crackers

Dinner: Whitefish with Wine and Peppercorns (pg 183 Heart Smart)
Green beans
Large Baked potato with no fat sour cream or Molly McButter

DAY 3

Breakfast: Bagel with no fat cream cheese
sliced banana with skim milk

Lunch: Ambrosia Fruit Salad (pg 104 Heart Smart)
hard roll (no more than 4 grams of fat)

Dinner: Turkey Lasagna (pg 201 Heart Smart)
Tossed Salad with low fat dressing

DAY 4

Breakfast: 1/3 cantaloupe
1 oz cereal with skim milk

Lunch: English muffin
2 oz tuna packed in water
mixed with no fat mayo
Melt no fat cheese on top if desired
Sliced pineapple

Dinner: Stuffed baked potato with cheese and broccoli
Applesauce
Celery/carrot sticks

DAY 5

Breakfast: 2 slices french toast made with egg beaters
3/4 cup fresh strawberries

Lunch: Gazpacho (pg 86 Heart Smart)
Roll or crackers

Dinner: Beef and Macaroni Casserole (pg 155 Heart Smart)
Fresh Asparagus

DAY 6

Breakfast: 3/4 c oatmeal with skim milk
raisins
Orange juice

Lunch: Herbed Chicken Salad (pg 100 Heart Smart)
Green grapes and 1/6 cantaloupe
Roll

Dinner: Spinach Calzones (pg 131 Heart Smart)
Sliced tomatoes and lettuce with low fat dressing

DAY 7

Breakfast: 2 EGGO waffles
1/2 c no-fat cottage cheese

Lunch: Shrimp and Rice Salad
Sliced orange

Dinner: Meatloaf
Baked Potato
Sliced carrots/Peas

DAY 8

Breakfast: 1 poached egg on toast
1/2 grapefruit

Lunch: Pita bread with leftover vegetables and no fat cheese
melted

Dinner: 6 Ounces broiled fish
pasta (angel hair or noodles)
1 cup steamed spinach

DAY 9

Breakfast: Breakfast Casserole

Lunch: Hearty Chicken Vegetable Soup (can)
4 saltine crackers
Apple

Dinner: Chicken Dijon
Rice
Broccoli

DAY 10

Breakfast: 3/4 c cold cereal with skim milk
1 piece of toast with jam
1/2 banana

Lunch: Pasta with low fat spaghetti sauce
Tossed Salad with low fat dressing

Dinner: Marinated Scallop Kabobs (pg 185 Heart Smart)
Rice

DAY 11

Breakfast: Shredded wheat cereal with skim milk
Strawberries

Lunch: Reuben sandwich:
1 oz canned corned beef
1/4 cup drained sauerkraut
1 oz low fat Swiss cheese
1 oz no fat Russian dressing

Dinner: Fettucini Parmesan with Vegetable (pg 193 Heart Smart)
Italian bread
Squash

DAY 12

Breakfast: Bagel with no fat cream cheese
1/2 grapefruit

Lunch: 1 cup clam chowder (canned)
crackers or roll
Pear

Dinner: Roast Turkey (slice and freeze in 3 ounce portions for lunches, etc.)
Sweet Potato
Brussels sprouts
Cranberry sauce

DAY 13

Breakfast: 3/4 cup oatmeal with skim milk
1/3 cantaloupe or honeydew

Lunch: Large wheat tortilla with deli turkey, lettuce, tomato
Microwave Potato Chips

Dinner: Chicken Hot Dog in roll
3/4 cup baked beans

DAY 14

Breakfast: Blueberry-Yogurt Muffin
1 boiled egg
Orange juice

Lunch: Greek salad with low fat dressing
Pita bread

Dinner: Stirfry chicken with broccoli and carrots
Rice pilaf
Mandarin oranges with pineapple chunks

DAY 15

Breakfast: Cold cereal of your choice with skim milk and 1/2 banana
Pineapple juice

Lunch: Grilled cheese (low fat cheese)
Sliced tomatoes with lettuce wedges, cucumbers

Dinner: Barbecue Chicken (pg 137 Heart Smart)
Noodles
Broccoli with cauliflower and carrots

DAY 16

Breakfast: Entenmann's coffee cake 1/2" slice
1/3 cantaloupe with no fat cottage cheese

Lunch: Sliced turkey sandwich with cranberry sauce

Dinner: Pasta Primavera
Green beans with mushrooms

DAY 17

Breakfast: 1 Apple Muffin
1/2 c cottage cheese

Lunch: Sliced cantaloupe and honeydew and strawberries
1 cup yogurt
Hard roll

Dinner: Corn chowder made with turkey
Corn bread

DAY 18

Breakfast: French toast made with egg beaters
Sliced peaches

Lunch: Ambrosia Fruit Salad (pg 104 Heart Smart)
Bed of lettuce
Choice of crackers

Dinner: Turkey Chili (pg 151 Heart Smart)
Corn bread with honey

DAY 19

Breakfast: 1/2 cantaloupe with cottage cheese and pineapple chunks
1/2 English muffin with jam

Lunch: Tuna Salad sandwich
Sliced tomato with lettuce with low fat dressing

Dinner: Pizza with Sauce Classico (pg 129 Heart Smart)
Tossed salad with low fat dressing (any fresh vegetables available)

DAY 20

Breakfast: Cream of wheat cereal with skim milk
Orange juice

Lunch: Healthy choice vegetable soup
Crackers
Apple

Dinner: Layered Cabbage/Beef Casserole (pg 168 Heart Smart)
Roll
Green Beans

DAY 21

Breakfast: 1 poached egg on toast
Cranberry juice

Lunch: Deli turkey sandwich on onion roll
Sliced tomato
Lettuce

Dinner: Stuffed peppers with either ground turkey or Healthy choice hamburg
Peas
Salad with low fat dressing

The *Heart Smart Cookbook* is filled with wonderful recipes and substitutions are encouraged.

Herbs and Seasonings will be a tremendous help in cooking the low fat way. Fresh herbs are always wonderful but dried herbs will serve most purposes of enhancing the dish to be served. Wine used for poaching adds flavor with no calories. Also, use no fat spray for stir frying of meats or vegetables.

Low Fat Desert Choices
Festive Fruitcake
All fresh fruits (no limit)
No Guilt Brownies
Frozen yogurt
Baked apples
Angel food cake
Cakes made with applesauce or crushed pineapple as substitute
    ingredients for oil
Puddings made with skim milk
Entenmann's no fat pound cake/oatmeal raisin cookies

Recipes

Egg Beaters Cheese Soufflé

¼ c butter or margarine (reduce to 3 T)
¼ c flour, scant
½ t salt
dash cayenne
1 c milk (may need a bit more)
8 oz Fat Free Cheese (about 10 slices)
1 box (8 oz) Egg Beaters
2 egg whites

Melt butter; blend in flour, salt and cayenne. Add milk all at once. Cook over medium heat, stirring until thick and bubbly. Remove from heat, Add cheese; stir until cheese melts (if too stiff add a bit more milk). Beat Egg Beaters. Slowly add cheese mixture, stirring constantly. Beat eggs to stiff peaks. Gradually pour eggbeater mixture over; fold together well. Pour into ungreased soufflé dish or casserole (2 qt.) Bake at 300° 1-1¼ hr. until knife inserted off-center comes out clean. Break apart into servings with 2 forks.

Yield: 4-6   3.4 grams fat per serving

Curried Lima Beans

2 pkg frozen baby lima beans
1 c water
2 T unsalted butter
1 medium onion, chopped (½ c)
4 t curry powder
¼ c plain yogurt
4 t lemon juice
¼ t salt
¼ t black pepper

Bring water and beans to boil in medium saucepan over high heat. Lower heat, cover and cook for 6 minutes. Drain beans, set aside. Melt butter in same saucepan over medium heat. Add onion and curry powder; cook, stirring occasionally, 6-8 minutes or until onion is tender. Stir in limas until heated through. Remove from heat. Stir in yogurt, lemon juice, salt and pepper until well combined and heated through. Serve immediately.

Yield: 4-6   3 grams fat per serving

Blueberry-Yogurt Muffins

2 c all-purpose flour
$1/3$ c sugar
1 t baking powder
1 t baking soda
¼ t salt
¼ c unsweetened orange juice
2 T vegetable oil
1 t vanilla extract
1 (8-oz) carton vanilla low-fat yogurt
1 egg
1 c fresh or frozen blueberries
Vegetable cooking spray
1 T sugar

Combine the first 5 ingredients in a large bowl; make a well in center of mixture.
Combine orange juice and next 4 ingredients; stir well. Add to dry ingredients, stirring just until moistened. Gently fold in blueberries. Divide batter evenly among 12 muffin cups coated with cooking spray; sprinkle 1 T sugar evenly over muffins. Bake at 400° for 18 minutes or until golden. Remove from pans immediately; let cool on a wire rack.

Yield: 1 dozen   3 grams fat per muffin

Chicken Dijon

6 chicken breasts split
3 T flour
1½-2 c chicken broth
¾ c non-fat sour cream
4 T Dijon mustard
2 tomatoes cut in wedges
2 T minced parsley

Brown chicken on both sides in broiler until well cooked. Remove to a platter and then make sauce with drippings, flour, sour cream and chicken broth to desired thickness. Put chicken back in pan and cook in 325° oven until all cooked and hot. Decorate with tomatoes and parsley to serve.

Yield: 12   8 grams fat each

French Market Soup

1 (12 oz) pkg dried bean soup
9 c water
1 c cubed lean cooked ham
½ t salt
¼ t white pepper
1 (16 oz) whole tomatoes
1½ c chopped onion
¾ c chopped celery
2 large cloves garlic, minced
3 T lemon juice
1 t hot sauce

Sort and wash bean soup mix; place in Dutch oven. cover with water 2 inches above beans; let soak 8 hours.

Drain beans and return to Dutch oven. Add 9 c water, ham, salt and white pepper.

Bring to a boil; reduce heat and simmer, uncovered, 2 hours or until beans are tender.

Chop tomatoes and add with remaining ingredients; simmer 30 minutes, stirring occasionally.

Yield: 6 servings (1½ c each).   2.9 grams fat per 1½ cups

No Guilt Brownies

3 oz unsweetened chocolate, chopped
1 c granulated sugar
¾ c flour
¾ c fat-free cottage cheese
3 egg whites
1 t salt
powdered sugar

Heat oven to 350°. Over very low heat, melt chocolate; cool slightly. In food processor, purée all ingredients except chocolate and powdered sugar until smooth. Add melted chocolate. Blend well. Pour into lightly buttered 8″ square pan. Bake 20-25 minutes or until just set. Sprinkle with powdered sugar. Cut into 16 squares.

1 gram fat per square

Cornmeal Yeast Muffins

1 pkg dry yeast
¼ c warm water (105-115°)
1⅓ c skim milk
⅓ c sugar
¼ c vegetable oil
¼ c margarine
1 t salt
½ c egg substitute
1½ c plain cornmeal
5-5½ c all-purpose flour, divided
Vegetable spray

Dissolve yeast in warm water in large bowl; let stand 5 minutes. Combine milk and next 4 ingredients in saucepan; cook over low heat until margarine melts. Cool to 105-115°. Add milk mixture to yeast mixture. Stir in egg substitute, corn meal, 2 c flour. Beat at medium speed with electric mixer until smooth. Stir in enough remaining flour to make a soft dough. Turn dough out onto a lightly floured surface and knead until smooth and elastic (about 8 min.). Place in a bowl coated with cooking spray, turning to grease top. Cover and let rise in warm place (85°), free from drafts, 1 hour or until doubled in bulk. Punch down dough; shape in 72 balls. Place 2 balls in muffin cup coated with spray. Let rise in warm place (85°), free from drafts, 45 min. or until doubled in bulk. Bake at 375° for 12-15 minutes or until golden. Coat muffins with cooking spray, remove from pans immediately. Serve or freeze.

Yield: 3 dozen   2.8 grams fat per muffin

Baked Apple

Large fresh apple
brown sugar
raisins (as desired)
sugar & cinnamon

Core apple, place in bowl. Sprinkle with cinnamon & sugar. Spoon brown sugar and raisins in opening. Microwave 3-4 minutes. May top with non-fat yogurt.

0 grams fat

Shrimp Stir-Fry with Ginger-Orange Sauce

1¼ lb medium-sized fresh unpeeled shrimp
vegetable cooking spray
4 c sliced yellow squash
1 c sliced zucchini
²/₃ c chopped red bell pepper
½ c diagonally sliced celery
½ lb pre-sliced fresh mushrooms
2 T cornstarch
1 T brown sugar
3 T reduced-sodium soy sauce
1 (10½ oz) can low-sodium chicken broth
2 cloves garlic, minced
2-3 t grated fresh gingerroot or ⅛ to ½ t ground ginger
6 c hot cooked rice (cooked without salt or fat)

Peel and devein shrimp. Coat a large non-stick skillet with cooking spray, and place over medium-high heat until hot. Add shrimp; stir-fry 2 minutes. Remove from skillet and set aside. Combine yellow squash, zucchini, bell pepper, celery and mushrooms; add half of vegetables to skillet. Stir-fry 3 min. over medium-high heat. Remove from skillet, and set aside. Repeat procedure with remaining vegetables; stir-fry 3 minutes and set aside. Combine cornstarch, brown sugar, soy sauce and chicken broth; stir well. Add garlic and ginger to skillet; sauté 30 seconds. Add cornstarch mixture; bring to a boil, stirring constantly. Cook 1 minute or until thickened. Stir in shrimp and vegetables; cook 1 minute. Serve over rice.

Yield: 6 servings (1 c shrimp mixture/1 c rice)   2.4 grams fat per serving

Turkey Tortilla

1 wheat tortilla
1 slice deli turkey
mustard or dijonaise
lettuce
sliced tomato

Spread mustard or dijonaise on tortilla. Add turkey and other ingredients as desired. Roll-up!

3 minute preparation   Yield: 1   1 gram fat

Breakfast Casserole

3 c cubed French bread
vegetable cooking spray
¾ c diced lean cooked ham
1 c (4 oz.) shredded, reduced fat sharp cheddar cheese
1¹/₃ c skim milk
¾ c egg substitute
¼ t dry mustard
¼ t onion powder
¼ t white pepper
paprika

Place bread evenly in 8″ square baking dish coated with cooking spray. Layer ham, red pepper and cheese over bread. Set aside. Combine next 4 ingredients; pour over cheese. Cover and refrigerate 8 hours. Remove from refrigerator; let stand 30 minutes. Bake, uncovered, at 350° for 30 minutes; sprinkle with paprika. Serve immediately.

Yield: 6 ¾-c servings   5 grams fat per serving

Meat Loaf

²/₃ c dry bread crumbs
1 c skim milk
1½ lbs ground turkey
½ c egg substitute
¼ t onion
1 t salt
½ t sage
pepper
Sauce
3 T brown sugar
¼ c catsup
¼ t nutmeg
1 t dry mustard

Mix all ingredients (except sauce) together well; mix sauce ingredients together. Pour sauce over meatloaf. Place in 350° oven for 45 minutes.

Yield: 4 servings   13 grams fat per serving

Shrimp and Rice Salad

3 c water
1 lb unpeeled, medium-size fresh shrimp
2 c cooked white rice
½ c chopped celery
½ c chopped green pepper
¼ c sliced pimento stuffed olives
¼ c chopped onion
2 T diced pimento
3 T oil-free Italian dressing
2 T reduced calorie or fat free mayonnaise
2 T prepared mustard
1 T lemon juice
1 t lemon-pepper seasoning
⅛ t pepper
Lettuce leaves

Bring water to boil; add shrimp and cook 3-5 minutes or until shrimp turns pink. Drain well; rinse with cold water. Chill. Peel and devein shrimp. Combine shrimp and next 6 ingredients in a medium bowl. Combine Italian dressing and next 5 ingredients, stirring until well blended. Pour over shrimp mixture, and toss gently to coat. Cover and chill 3-4 hours. Line a serving plate with lettuce leaves. Spoon salad onto plate.

Yield: 5 1-c servings   3.1 grams fat per serving

3 oz. Chicken Breasts

Season with herbs as desired. Pour ⅓ c chablis over in pan. Simmer 3-4 minutes, turning once. Serve with rice, pasta or baked potato.

4-6 grams fat

Festive Fruitcake

¼ c brandy
1 (6 oz) can frozen unsweetened orange juice concentrate,
    thawed and undiluted
1 c fresh cranberries, chopped
1 (8 oz) package pitted dates, chopped
1 c chopped pecans
1 T grated orange rind
1 t vanilla extract
½ c egg substitute
1 (8 oz) can unsweetened pineapple tidbits, drained
2 c all-purpose flour
1¼ t baking soda
¼ t salt
½ t cinnamon
¼ t nutmeg
¼ t allspice
vegetable cooking spray
½ c brandy
3 T apple brandy

Combine first 3 ingredients in large bowl; cover and let stand 1 hour. Combine dates and next 5 ingredients; stir into cranberry mixture. Combine flour and next 5 ingredients. Stir into fruit mixture. Spoon batter into a 6-cup Bundt or tube pan coated with cooking spray; bake at 325° for 45 minutes or until wooden pick inserted in center of cake comes out clean. Cool in pan on wire rack 20 minutes; remove from pan and let cool completely on wire rack. Bring ½ c brandy to boil; cool. Moisten several layers of cheese cloth with brandy and wrap cake. Cover with plastic wrap, then aluminum foil. Store in a cool place at least 1 week, or freeze up to 3 months. Before serving, melt apple jelly in a saucepan over low heat, stirring constantly. Brush over cake.

Yield: 21 servings   4.1 grams fat per serving

Tortillas

2 flour tortillas
4 T saucepan beans
Salsa of choice
non-fat sour cream
2 slices non-fat cheese

Put 2 T of beans and a generous portion of salsa in each tortilla and roll. Lay 1 slice of cheese on each tortilla. Add more salsa or microwave about 1.5 minutes. Add dollup of sour cream. Enjoy with a handful (approx. 26) of guiltless tortilla chips.

Yield: 2 servings   4.5 grams fat per serving

Mexican Rice and Beans

1 t canola oil
½ c water
1 onion chopped
2 cloves garlic, minced
1½ c mushrooms, sliced
2 sweet peppers, chopped
¾ c long-grain rice
1 can (28 oz) red kidney beans, drained
1 can (19 oz) tomatoes
1 T chili powder
2 t cumin
¼ t cayenne pepper
1 c shredded low-fat mozzarella cheese
Optional
1 small can whole kernel corn
¼ c red wine

In large skillet or Dutch oven, heat oil with water over medium heat. Add onion, garlic, mushrooms and green peppers; simmer, stirring often, until onion is tender, about 10 minutes. Add rice, beans, tomatoes, chili powder, cumin and cayenne (also optional items). Simmer 25 minutes or until rice is tender and most of the liquid is absorbed. Transfer to baking dish and sprinkle with cheese. Bake in 350° oven for 15 minutes or micowave on high for 1-2 minutes or until cheese melts.

Yield: 6 1-c servings.   5 grams fat per serving

Corn Chowder

2 T margarine
1 c chicken boullion
2 medium onions
2 cloves garlic, chopped
½ c celery, chopped
1 pepper, chopped, seeds & membranes removed
1 lb ground turkey
1½ t cayenne pepper
1½ t fennel seed, crushed
1 t coarse ground pepper
6 medium potatoes, raw, pared & diced
4 c chicken boullion or stock
½ t salt
½ t paprika
2 bay leaves
3 c skim milk
3 16-oz cans of whole kernel corn, drained
1 c instant potato buds

In margarine and boullion, saute onions, garlic, celery and pepper. Add ground turkey, cayenne pepper, fennel seed and pepper. Saute until brown and any liquid is gone. Add potatoes, boullion, salt, paprika and bay leaves. In separate saucepan, combine until blended skim milk and corn and bring to the boiling point. When potatoes are tender (about 45 minutes), add this milk mixture to base. Reheat, but do not boil. Slowly add potato buds (1 c more or less) until desired consistency is achieved. Stir until smooth.

Yield: 12-14 servings.   Approx. 4 grams fat per serving

Microwave Potato Chips

Unpeeled potatoes

Slice potatoes very thinly. Use 9 X 13 pyrex pan upside down. Spray with Pam. Cover with potato slices and sprinkle with salt. Cook on high for 4-7 minutes until light brown. Cool one minute.

0 grams fat

Pasta Primavera

3 c broccoli florets, cut into bite-sized pieces
½ lb fresh mushrooms, quartered
2 small zucchini, sliced into ¼" rounds
1 T olive oil
3 cloves garlic, minced
1 pt cherry tomatoes, stemmed and cut in half
8 oz fettucine
Sauce
¾ c skim milk
3 T nonfat "butter" granules (i.e. Molly McButter)
²/₃ c part-skim ricotta cheese
¼ c grated Parmesan cheese
2 T chopped fresh basil or 1 T dried basil
¼ c dry sherry

Steam broccoli, mushrooms and zucchini for 3 minutes or until just tender. Set aside. In large nonstick skillet or wok, heat olive oil over medium-high heat. Add garlic and sauté for 1 minute, stirring frequently. Add tomatoes and sauté for 2 minutes, stirring frequently until tomatoes are slightly cooked, but not wilted. Set aside. Cook fettucine according to package directions, omitting salt. Drain well. Combine milk, "butter" granules, ricotta cheese, parmesan cheese, basil and sherry in blender. Process until smooth. In small saucepan, heat sauce over low heat, stirring frequently, until warm. In large serving dish, toss drained pasta, vegetables and sauce to coat well. Garnish each portion with Parmesan cheese and pepper. Serve immediately.

Yield: 4 2-cup servings.   2 grams fat per serving

Apple Muffins

2 c all-purpose flour
¼ c plus 2 T firmly packed brown sugar
1 t baking powder
½ t baking soda
½ t ground cinnamon
¼ t salt
1½ c peeled, shredded Rome apples
$^1/_3$ c plus 2 T nonfat buttermilk
2 T vegetable oil
1 t vanilla extract
1 egg
Vegetable cooking spray

Combine first 6 ingredients in large bowl; make well in center of mixture. Combine apple and next 4 ingredients; stir well. Add to dry ingredients, stirring until just moistened. Divide batter evenly among 12 muffin cups coated with cooking spray. Bake at 400° for 28 minutes or until a wooden pick inserted in center comes out clean. Remove from pans immediately; let cool on wire rack.

Yield: 1 dozen (Serving size 1 muffin)   3.2 grams fat

Discipline

*For the moment all discipline seems painful
rather than pleasant. Later it yields the
peaceful fruits of righteousness to those who
have been trained by it.*

Hebrews 12:11

he second emphasis in this program is on discipline. So often the word discipline connotes a negative response in us, and we forget that it is a positive action necessary for Christian growth. Hebrews tells us that discipline is painful rather than pleasant (for the moment), but it promises to produce the fruit of righteousness to those of us who will be trained by it (Heb. 12:11).

Take a new look at the word discipline and let God change your opinion about it. It will set you free.

Since God desires us to lead well-ordered and disciplined lives, the disciplines of the 3D program will serve as tools to help you develop new habit patterns in prayer, Bible study, eating, work, use of time and caring for others. Each discipline is an important part of 3D's goal to help you become the person God wants you to be.

Prayer

Daily prayer will help you develop a closer relationship with God. Praying consistently at a regular time each day will help reinforce your prayer discipline. It only takes a minute or two to bring ten names to the Lord. He knows their specific needs, but praying for others deeply blesses us in the process. If you are in a group, pray for the other members as well as the leaders every day for twelve weeks. You will be amazed at how exciting it is to be a small part of what God does for the members of the group. If you are doing 3D alone, pray for five people you know (other than family). Make a commitment to God to faithfully pray for them each day.

"My Prayer List"

1.
2.
3.
4.
5.

This is also a good time to pray for your family, your church, the country, your personal needs, and other concerns which the Lord may bring to mind. Pray expectantly—God's answers are exciting!

Attendance at Group Meetings

Faithful weekly attendance is an important element of your commitment to the program. Since the 3D group is a safe place in which inner conflicts can be faced, exposed, fought and healed, the support of the group is vital.

If you are doing this program on your own, it would be our recommendation that you decide before starting the twelve weeks the day and time of the week you are going to weigh yourself. Also, remember to set a daily specific time for your prayer, daily devotional reading and Bible study. This will require discipline on your part since you do not have the support of a group around you.

Daily Devotional Readings and Bible Study

Daily devotional readings and Bible study questions are a very important part of the 3D program. Whenever we deny ourselves, whether it be by being on a diet or getting up in the morning earlier than usual, we find ourselves more rebellious than we even imagined. Being "fed" spiritually by daily devotions, Bible reading and Bible study is a vital part of what God wants to do for you during these next twelve weeks. Don't miss this part of the program. Your workbook is included in this packet.

The Food Sheet

Each day record all that you eat on your food sheet. We would encourage you to record each meal as you eat rather than once a day. The food sheet should be turned into the 3D leaders at your group meeting time.

There is a possibility that you have never been this honest about your eating habits. We pray that this record will show you the trouble spots in your day and where you need to change. Then you can ask Jesus to help you.

This food sheet can be a valuable tool even if you are not interested in losing weight. It helps you see weak areas in your eating patterns and where you are not receiving good nutrition.

It is also an excellent tool for anyone suffering from eating disorders.

Menu Planning

Menu planning is an area where discipline is frequently lacking. Too often a family eats meals that reflect the mood of the cook. Do not allow poor preparation or planning to be an excuse for disobedience. You will be blessed by a carefully planned menu.

God is concerned about your stewardship in the use of money and time. By making out a menu and shopping list ahead of time, you can check advertisements and clip coupons. Include specials in the menus to help keep within your food budget.

Bible Memorization

The Psalmist said, "I have laid up Thy word in my heart, that I might not sin against thee." (Psalm 119:11)

The Word of God will strengthen, encourage, and protect you as you face the problems and temptations of daily living. To help you put God's Word in your heart, Bible memorization is part of 3D. Each week memorize the verse corresponding to the lesson of the week, and then commit it to your heart so that you may practice it daily. The verse is found at the beginning of each week in your devotional workbook.

Caring for Another

Too often we become concerned with our own problems, which grow out of proportion and are overwhelming. Serving and caring for others helps us keep our problems in perspective. One telephone call or a visit with someone each week is a way to begin this.

Be open to the prompting of the Holy Spirit in making telephone calls. He can show you whom to call and when to make the call. We encourage people in 3D to make one "caring" call each week, or a visit. Be sensitive to the time of day you make your call, and the length of each conversation. *Don't talk too long!*

Try to serve others in your contacts with those in your group and don't hesitate to share your own needs in these conversations.

If you are doing 3D on your own, ask the Lord to lead you in a caring deed every week for someone else. It can be a phone call, or a letter to someone, or a visit to a shut-in.

A Sample Food Sheet —

3D *Food Sheet* Name Susan Daily Calories 1200 Week Beginning: NOW

Meal	Group	MODEL	1	2	3	4	5	6	7
BREAKFAST	MEAT	1	1 soft boiled egg	1 cottage cheese	1	1 Peanut butter	1 eggs	1 1oz. cheese	1
	BREAD	1	1 ½ Eng. muffin	1 1 slice toast	1 Fr. toast	1 ¾ c. shredded wheat	1 toast	1 oatmeal	1 Fr. toast
	FRUIT	1	1 ½ grapefruit	1 ¼ cantaloupe	1 ½ c. OJ	1 ½ banana	1 ½ c. g.fruit juice	1 apple	1 ½ c. pineapple
	MILK	½	½ ½ c milk	½ ½ c. milk	½ ½ c. milk	½ ½ c. milk	½ ½ c. milk	½ ½ c. milk	½ ½ c. milk
	FAT	1	1 1 tsp. marg.	1	1	1 PB	1	1 1oz. mayo	1 1 t. marg.
	FREE								
	SNACK								
LUNCH	MEAT	2	2 ¼ c. tuna	2 Sp. Omelet	2 1oz. meat cheese	2 2oz. turkey	2 cottage cheese	2 2oz. hamburger	2 Peanut butter
	BREAD	2	2 2 pieces toast	2 2½ Eng. muffins	2 12 crackers	2 cabbage	2 6 melba toast	2 1 roll	2 12 crackers tomato soup
	VEGETABLE	2	2 salad	2 green beans	2 salad	2 lettuce	2 V8 juice	2 tomato/cucumbers	2 lettuce
	FRUIT	1	1 apple	1 grapes	1 ½ banana	1 tangerine	1 pineapple	1 ½ grapefruit	1 ½ banana
	MILK	1	1 1c. milk	1 1c. milk	1	1 1c. milk	1 1c. milk	1 1c. milk	1 1c. milk
	FAT	2	2 2t. marg.	2 2 t. marg.	2	2 mayo	2 2t. marg.	2	2 PB
	FREE								
	SNACK								
DINNER	MEAT	2	2 2oz. chicken	2 2oz. fish	2 Pork Belgian	2 Beef Stew	2 2oz. turkey	2 Chicken Crepes	2 Beef
	BREAD	1	1 ½ c. rice	1 potato	1 Potatoes	1 Potatoe	1 ½ c. potato	1 crepes	1 ⅓ c. rice
	VEGETABLE	2	2 ½ c. carrots ½ c. beans	2 spinach	2 beets	2	2 beans/carrots	2 ½ c. peas	2 brocoli
	FRUIT	1	1 orange	1 jello	1 applesauce	1 fruitcup	1 strawberries	1 orange	1 pears
	MILK	½	½ ½ c. milk	½ ½ c. milk	½ ½ c. milk	½ ½ c. milk	½ ½ c. milk	½ ½ c. milk	½ ½ c. milk
	FAT	1	1 1 t. marg.	1 1 t. marg.	1 1 t. marg.	1 stew	1 1 t. marg.	1 crepes	1t. marg.
	FREE								
	SNACK								

3D and Exercise

3D is concerned about the whole area of exercise—not only for weight loss but for overall good health purposes. However, we also feel exercise can be overdone and needs to be carefully considered for each individual. With this in mind, 3D has included a stretching, strengthening and toning exercise tape in Action Kit I.

"What good is it to lose weight if it's just going to come back? The goal is to lose fat! Exercise, along with the proper diet, will help you do that."

—*Ed Haver*

The Lasting Benefits of Exercise

Ed Haver, M.S.
Certified Program Director of American College of Sports Medicine
Special Exercise Consultant to 3D

As you look to the future, I hope that you see exercise as an integral part of your healthy lifestyle. A regular habit of exercise is very important, not only to your overall well-being, but also to success in keeping your weight at an optimum level. The major dilemma we normally face is not rapid weight gain but what has been termed "creeping obesity." One hundred extra calories a day doesn't sound like much, but over the course of a year it means an extra ten pounds. Walk an extra mile a day and you will take care of the extra one hundred calories. And the side benefits are even better: improved cardiovascular efficiency, increased energy to do normal tasks, released tensions, and toned muscles, to mention just a few. Don't settle for anything but the best, especially when such a small investment of time can return such tremendous dividends.

The New Testament contains several passages comparing exercise and the Christian life. The pursuit of fitness and Christian maturity both require regular daily times of discipline. To be successful in the pursuit of fitness you have to make increased activity a part of your life. As you study the life of Jesus, you find no examples of structured exercise periods, yet how many of us could walk from Galilee to Jerusalem (75 miles one way), as He often did? For that matter, how many of us could walk from Jerusalem up the hill to the Garden of Gethsemane?

In today's mechanized world, it is important to have that structured exercise time, but also try to find ways to be more active during your normal routine: walk whenever you have a chance, climb the stairs when possible, stretch and reach throughout the day. It takes creativity and planning to put together a program that is just right for you. Don't get discouraged about what you can't do, but instead get excited about what you can do.

If you find that your exercise becomes sporadic, stop and analyze the reasons why. Getting up at 6 A.M. might have been fine during the summer—but bring on the dark and cold of winter and motivation can wear thin. Can you plug in some activity at lunchtime, or possibly in the afternoon? Or maybe you know someone in the same dilemma—arrange to meet each other in the early hours and your motivation will perk up. Don't let minor problems sidetrack your efforts—look at them as opportunities to be creative.

Keep in mind *that the best types of activities for burning calories and helping your cardiovascular system are those that require at least 20-30 minutes of sustained effort.* Keep a check on your pulse to make sure it stays in your target range if you also want to give your heart and lungs a workout. Try to get out at least every other day for a minimum of twenty minutes and your body will reward you by functioning as God intended.

Remember to always stretch before and after you exercise (just a few minutes) and then warm up gradually. When you get to the end of your exercise period, don't forget to cool down by simply slowing down whatever you are doing. This is very important, as most exercise-induced problems occur due to lack of a proper cool-down.

Hopefully you have become more and more acquainted with the inner workings of your body the past few months. Learn to listen to what it is telling you—by all means don't push it too far, too quickly. Take it easy and gradually make changes, allowing it time to adapt—and adapt it will. Give your body the activity it craves and soon you will become "positively addicted" to exercise. If you do get signals that don't seem right (pain in the joints, chest pain, extreme breathlessness, etc.) do visit your doctor and make sure that the form of exercise you've selected is best for you.

There are no magical methods or hidden shortcuts to physical fitness—just regular consistent work. I am convinced that the Lord wants His people to have bodies that function as He designed them. Therefore if you find yourself having trouble getting going, let Jesus know about it. If you really want to please Him, then He will give you the power to carry out your good intentions. Talk to Him about it and then get moving—He'll keep you going. What happens to the Lord's temple is up to you. Be a good landlord—your Tenant deserves the very best you have to offer!

Exercise for Beginners

What kind of visual picture do you get when you hear the word "exercise?" Do you see people sweating, panting and pushing until they are close to collapse? Or, do you picture a Marine drill sergeant barking out, "one, two, three, four . . . " as you try to keep up with calisthenics that must have come from a book of medieval tortures. As you read this, I'd like to have you clear your head of any negative thoughts that you might have about it. Be sure to hang on to any positive ones, and for the next few minutes let me convince you that exercise is the greatest thing since sliced bread.

The human body was made to be active. When God programmed our bodies, He made them function at their peak efficiency in an environment of movement. With our modern technology, we have numerous labor-saving devices which, while saving us time, have ruined our health. Therefore, we are experiencing an epidemic of diseases which are the result of disuse and misuse of the body. Coronary heart disease is a major culprit in this attack. More people die of coronary heart disease than from all other causes of death combined. A regular, sensible program of exercise has been shown to help reduce many of the primary risk factors of heart disease. Exercise will help stabilize your blood pressure, reduce stress, increase your heart efficiency, allow you to sleep better, give you more energy and generally put more life into your years. Sagging, flabby muscles will be toned up as your body begins to function in the way God designed, and your weight will begin to come under control as you burn excess fat as energy to fuel your increasingly active lifestyle.

Losing Fat Instead of Muscle

What about exercise and weight control? This is an area that I am really excited about, as I've personally seen many people who have fought weight problems for years, finally gain success as they begin to incorporate exercise into their lives.

Let's look at this area a little more closely. When a person goes on a low-calorie diet, many things happen. One is that the person loses weight. But what type of weight is it? You probably didn't know that you can lose the wrong type of weight. Your body composition can generally be divided into two major categories: lean body weight—

that's muscles, bones, organs, and that awful stuff . . . **fat**! When you strictly diet, usually up to half of the weight you lose is lean body weight. That means that you are decreasing your muscle weight—weight which you normally want to conserve. As your weight drops, you tend to tire out easily, your muscle tone slackens and you feel generally weak. Immediately upon returning to a normal diet, much of this lean body weight is built back up and most of your hard earned weight loss is gained back. Add a sensible exercise program to your diet, and you will lose primarily fat—normally around 90%. Now when you get to your goal weight, you're ready to stay there and you haven't lost your strength. What good is it to lose weight if it's just going to come back? The goal is to lose fat! Exercise along with the proper diet, will help you do that.

The Basal Metabolism Rate—How It Works

As you strictly diet, you also can greatly affect what is called your basal metabolic rate, or your BMR. Your BMR is that rate at which your body burns calories while you are at rest. These are used to keep all of the body functions going. As you limit your caloric intake, your BMR will decrease as your body works to preserve itself. In extreme cases, even your hair will stop growing as your body works to conserve energy. Therefore, the low-calorie diet that has you losing pounds at the beginning, a few weeks later might simply maintain your weight. I can't think of anything that is more discouraging than to work hard counting calories only to have your body work just as hard to decrease how many it burns. The solution—you guessed it—exercise. You need to increase your BMR and one of the best ways to do this is by exercising. This relates directly to one of the main misunderstandings about exercise—that it takes a lot of exercise to have any effect on weight loss. Theoretically it does take 35 miles of walking to burn one pound of fat. Now this is based on the fact that you burn about 100 calories per mile of walking—that a pound of fat is 3500 calories of energy. Now that sounds discouraging! What this doesn't take into account is the fact that every time you exercise, you elevate your metabolic rate. So exercise does have a long term effect. You not only burn calories for the time you exercise, but, if done correctly, for a period of time after you exercise you continue to elevate your basal metabolic rate beyond the time of the actual exercise. So, if you walk after dinner, you will burn extra calories while you sleep.

Loungers vs. Exercisers

"But how about my increased appetite?" you might ask. Many studies have looked at this area and in one famous study—the caloric intake of two sets of rats were compared. Both sets were given all the food they wanted with the only difference being their activity levels. One set of rats was exercised one hour per day on an exercise wheel, while the other set just lounged around. *The "loungers" ate more food than the "exercisers."* If a rancher wants to fatten up a steer for market, does he let him run free or does he pen him up? Keep him fenced in, he'll eat more and soon you'll have a nice fat steer. Let him run and he'll be lean and tough. If you exercise following the basic guidelines that I'll go into next, your appetite will not be increased by the activity, but be aware of the reward system . . . walk a mile, eat a candy bar! . . . walk two miles, eat a piece of pie! . . . walk six miles, eat a *whole pie!* Don't let your brain mislead you.

Finding the Right Exercise

When most people think of exercise, they think of *calisthenics,* but the best exercises for weight loss and overall health are the aerobic exercises. Aerobic means "with oxygen" or a sustained effort designed primarily to exercise the heart and the lungs. Good examples are activities such as walking, bicycle riding, swimming, or jogging which burn numerous calories while improving your fitness. The problem with these exercises comes in knowing how fast to go, how far to keep going, and how often to get out and do it.

First, let's talk about how fast you should exercise. The intensity at which you exercise is *very* important. I have found, in working with people who are beginning exercise programs, that most of them go too fast. An example is jogging vs. walking. For some reason, most people feel that they *have* to jog to do themselves any good. This is just not true. Walking is tremendous activity. More about that later. Exercise too fast and you're more prone to injuries, you won't enjoy it as much and you'll primarily use muscle instead of fat for fuel.

Now let's talk about some basic guidelines that you can use to help you determine the proper intensity for your exercise. The formulas that I'm going to give you are very general. You should use them only as guidelines and let your body then make the necessary changes. We will use your heart rate, your pulse, to measure how hard you are working. Basically, you should increase your heart rate to about 75% of your maximum. To do this, first you need to determine your maximum heart rate. There are three methods of doing this: one way is to find a *big* hill and a person who can count quickly. You run up the hill as fast as you can and when you collapse, your friends takes your pulse rate. The use of this method is *strongly* discouraged! *Please don't do it!*

The second method involves having a stress test or an exercise EKG. This is somewhat similar to Method No. 1 except there is a cardiologist nearby and the test is done on a treadmill.

The last method will help you arrive at your maximum heart rate, your resting heart rate and your training heart rate.

MAXIMUM: Subtract your age from the number 220 to determine this rate. Be sure that you memorize your maximum heart rate and never exceed it!

RESTING: Count your heart rate (pulse) a full minute at a time when your heart is working the least. Use either the pulse in your wrist or the carotid artery in your neck.

TRAINING: Multiply your maximum rate by 60 percent, 75 percent and 85 percent to find the lowest, middle, and upper ranges of intensity for your own exercise program. An effective aerobic program should raise your rate to 75 percent of the maximum. However, when you first begin your exercise program you will notice your pulse rate will be about 60% of the maximum heart rate. This will increase as you become more fit. You should take your pulse rate for ten seconds immediately following your exercise. Multiply this by 6 to find out your heart rate per minute. It would be a good idea to check your rate at 10 minute intervals as you exercise in the beginning.

Checking Your Pulse

Before we get to that point, you need to know how to monitor your pulse. There are two main sites. One good site is the radial artery which runs along your wrist on the thumb side. Using two fingers (not your thumb) you can feel for this pulse. Press at different spots and don't press too hard. Then looking at a watch with a second hand, count all of the beats that occur in 10 seconds. Now if you have difficulty finding your pulse here (which happens)—then try the next spot. Large caratoid arteries run up both sides of your neck to your brain. If you feel over from your windpipe, you should be able to locate this artery. It's a main artery. Two major points here: (1) don't press on both sides at the same time or you'll get a *real close* view of the floor, and (2) don't press up high on your neck. Find it down low and press lightly. This artery is usually more prominant and fairly easy to locate. That's enough theory.

Gauging Your Speed

The next step is go out and exercise at what you consider a good pace. You can walk, jog, bicycle, swim, bounce on a mini trampoline or a rebounder or any activity that will increase your heart rate. After two to three minutes, stop and take your ten-second pulse. You'll probably find now that it is a lot easier to locate that pulse. Compare this number to the number we just came up with. If your heart rate is supposed to get to 20 and you find that yours is at 24, then slow down. If it's at 16, speed up a bit. Continue to exercise and keep monitoring your pulse. At first you will need to take it about every five minutes. Gradually you'll begin to know what it feels like when you are at the correct pace and you'll only need to take it in the beginning, maybe the middle and at the end. Now this pace will vary for everyone. Therefore, watch your pulse, do what you should do and don't worry about anyone else. For some people, this will be an easy walk, for some people it will be a jog. Concentrate on your pulse. Do what's right for you. Knowing your intensity, we can move on to the next questions.

How far and how often? To help improve your cardiovascular system, you should maintain this heart rate for a minimum of 20 minutes four times per week. These are minimums for increasing and then maintaining your fitness at a good level. Keep your intensity where it should be and the 20 minutes will go by rapidly.

Frequency and Length Rather Than Speed

In terms of weight control and/or weight loss, these two areas are key. The longer you can exercise, the more calories you burn, and it's the same with frequency. These are the two areas you should emphasize. Again, don't worry too much about speed. I would much rather have you slow down and go longer. In terms of calories, you burn almost the same if you jog a mile or walk a mile. Also, work on increasing how often you exercise. Now any exercise that meets these three requirements is a good cardiovascular exercise. That is, it increases your heart rate to approximately 75% of your maximum, if continued for at least 20 minutes and you can do it at least four times a week. You don't have to do the same exercise every day either. Be creative. Swim one day, ride a bicycle, but again, whatever you do, follow these same basic guidelines as to intensity, duration and frequency. That might sound a bit complex, but I think as you work through it, you find your pulse number, and then you start to practice it, you'll find it to be very easy and very helpful.

Calories Burned per Activity

Activity	Calories extended per hour	
	Women	Men
Sitting quietly	80	100
Standing quietly	95	120

Light Activity
  Cleaning house
  Office work
  Playing golf
	240	300

Moderate Activity
  Walking briskly (3.5 mph)
  Gardening
  Cycling (5.5 mph)
	370	460

Strenuous Activity Jogging (9 min/mile)	580	920
Healthy women—140 lbs. Healthy men-175 lbs. These are approximate. Vary according to environmental conditions.		

Some Other Points to Remember

Now as you begin, there are a few other major points you should remember.

First, if you haven't done much regular exercise recently, *please* check with your doctor before you begin. This might sound like the typical line—and it is, but it's important. Exercise is similar to taking medication. It can really help, but you have to follow the guidelines to minimize the risk and maximize the benefits. Check with your doctor if you have any questions.

Every exercise session should have three parts to it. *First,* you need to warm up. Just like your car needs to start slowly in the morning, so do you. Once you're warmed up, you can "cruise" through your 20, 30, 45 minutes of exercise at your correct heart rate. After that comes the most critical time in exercising—the "cool down." After a horse race, do the trainers put the horses back in the stalls? Of course not. They walk them out. Similarly, you need to gradually return your heart rate and blood pressure to near pre-exercise levels. As you exercise, a large amount of blood is pumped through your legs. This blood returns to the heart via the veins. The veins have one-way valves that open when the muscles squeeze on them. These close when the muscle relaxes. Therefore, the blood returns very efficiently while you exercise. But if you stop suddenly, you greatly diminish the blood return and you put a tremendous load on your heart. Your blood pressure might drop very quickly, resulting in dizziness, fainting, and/or irregular heart rhythm. At the YMCAs and the health clubs, the majority of exercise related heart problems don't occur on the track or the bicycles, but in the shower rooms and in the parking lots. So, take three to five minutes and *gradually* slow down, so when you do stop, it won't be a shock to your system. *Very important point to remember!*

Next, step back and look at your schedule. Think about your priorities, and gradually begin to increase your activity patterns. Besides your set exercise time, look for other times to be active. Park further from the market or work, and walk. Take the stairs when you can. Get the mid-afternoon "blahs?" . . . try a brisk walk instead of a nap. The calories burned will add up and your weight will go down. But more importantly, you'll have the energy to do all that you want.

As you begin, there are a few tips that might help you be successful.

First off, plan ahead. If you plan to come home tomorrow afternoon and walk and you have dinner guests coming, it's going to be tough. Most of the people who come through our programs find the morning to be the best time for them to exercise. It's quiet, there's less pollution, and primarily, there are fewer interruptions. How many people call you at 6:30 in the morning? But on the other hand, maybe you are not a morning person. You might find exercising on your lunch hour or getting out of the house to relax during the late afternoon suits you better, and that's fine. But whenever, plan ahead. If you're going to walk in the morning, be sure to get everything out the night before . . . clothes, shoes, socks, whatever, and have it all ready to go. Then the idea is to get up, get dressed and out the door before your brain wakes up. The hardest part is getting out the door. So, make it as easy as possible. The best idea to get you going is to find someone to exercise with you. They will get there on time for you, and you'll get there for them. This is the number one way to guarantee success. Remember, start easy, be regular and stick with it . . . I'm sure you'll like the results.

A Daily Walk

Another practical exercise program is to start WALKING. Walking is a tremendous form of exercise and one in which everyone can participate. It is good for every part of your body. Walk twenty minutes and burn available calories. After that short period of time you begin to use fat as fuel. Once fat burning is initiated, the basic metabolic rate goes up for the rest of your walk, and can stay up for several hours after you stop. Many experts in the exercise field believe that sustained slow exercise burns fat often more effectively than intense fast exercise which tends to break down your muscles. To walk for fitness does mean something different than strolling. Brisk, sustained, walking 3-5 times a week for 20-30 minutes is a good walking program.

Walking can be a wonderful blessing to you. It can perk up your spirit, relax your nerves. It is incredible how problems can vanish or work themselves out as you walk. If you look around and see the trees, the birds, the clouds, a bunch of berries peeking out of the bushes, somehow a smile comes to your face and in your heart and frustrated feelings seem to disappear. It is a wonderful time to pray and think about all God has given you. It is a perfect time to pray for family and friends (and members of your Time To Grow class). A walk can be the turning point in your day in more ways than one. If you walk one mile every day for a year you will lose 10 pounds.

In summary we want to mention the areas that will be helped by a regular exercise program:

> the heart
> circulation
> breathing
> digestion, elimination
> posture and balance
> bones, muscles, ligaments, and tendons
> sleep/relaxation
> stress
> body weight

Marjorie Holmes says "Exercise tells the body it's appreciated, worthy of our attention. Exercise tells the body, and its Creator 'Thank you, I love you.' And the body responds. Not only physically but spiritually, with a feeling of well-being, of peace and delight and self-respect."

A Good Warm-up

Now as I mentioned earlier, part of a good warm-up should include some stretching exercises. These exercises will increase your flexibility, cut down on injuries, and prepare your muscles and joints for exercise. The following seven exercises will take about four minutes to complete and I *strongly* urge that you do them at least before you exercise. After exercising is also very helpful. On all of the stretches, it's important that you do an *easy* stretch and don't bounce. When you feel it start to pull, ease off just a bit and then *hold* it in that position for the time advised. Make sure you hold it for long enough. It takes patience, but it is *very important.* You can gain a lot without having to strain and hurt.

Exercises
Warm-Ups

1. Head Rolls: Drop your head and rotate right, back, left and forward. Repeat. Then reverse and do same movement to the left two times.

2. Shoulder Rolls: Lift and rotate right shoulder back, lift and rotate left shoulder back, lift and rotate both shoulders back together. Repeat for a total of four times.

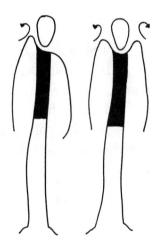

3. Reach to Heaven: Raise right arm over head, left arm down at your side, stretch and extend the right arm. Then switch and repeat the stretch and extend movement with the left arm up and right arm down. Repeat for a total of eight.

4. Waist Rolls: Place hands on hips, legs shoulder width apart. Bend forward at the waist, rotate body right, back, left and forward. Repeat. Then reverse and rotate body left, back, right and forward. Repeat.

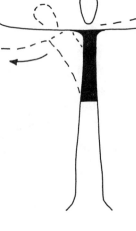

5. Lean Stretch: Stand up straight, with feet shoulder width apart, and extend arms shoulder height with palms facing out toward the walls. Alternate pushing toward the wall with palms by leaning first right, then left. Alternate this movement for a total of eight.

6. Slide Stretch: Keep feet shoulder width apart, arms down at sides, bend to the right and slide arm down right leg, while left arm slides up. Repeat to the left. Do this exercise alternating sides for a total of eight. Remember to keep your stomach muscles pulled in tightly.

7. Heel Stretch: Stand with the left leg forward, knee bent, and right leg stretched behind as far back as needed to feel a stretch in the calf. The further behind the body you place the right leg, the greater the stretch. Then, raise and lower the right heel, stretching the calf muscle as you come down. Do eight of these. Switch legs repeating the exercise with right leg forward, knee bent, and left leg behind for a total of eight.

8. Wake Up Praise: Place palms together, lift arms up over head then separate and lower to sides as you bend over and sweep the floor. Repeat for a total of four.

Warm-Ups

1. Jogging in place.

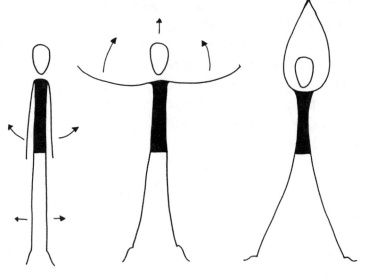

2. Jumping Jacks.

3. Jogging in place with Body Twists.   4. Jogging with Heels up.

5 Jogging in Place with Knees up.

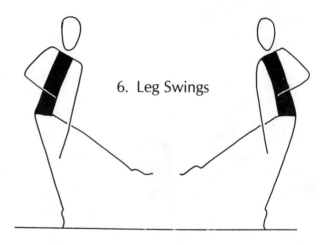

6. Leg Swings

7. Walk Heel-Toe Slowly

8. Praise Stretch

9. Heel Stretch

10. Body Rolls

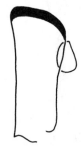

11. Rag Doll Shake

Arms

1. Small and Large Arm Circles: Stand with feet shoulder width apart, extend arms shoulder height and make 8 small circles forward and 8 small circles backwards and repeat. Follow this by making 4 large circles forward and 4 large circles backwards and repeat.

2. Scissors: Starting in a bent-over position, count to eight while making a scissoring motion with arms, moving your body into a standing position with arms then up and over your head, then back down again to a count of 8 and repeat.

3. Wing Stretches: Stand up straight and begin by bending arms so that fingers just touch at chest level. Stretch elbows back and then extend straightened arms back. There are two movements to each wing stretch and we do sixteen.

Waist

1. Wrap Arounds: Feet shoulder width apart, extend arms and twist upper body to the right, wrapping the left arm around your waist. Twist left and wrap right arm around waist. Continue to alternate sides and do sixteen.

2. Waist Reaches: Pull stomach muscles tight, feet shoulder width apart and stretch left arm over head to the right and curve the right arm to the left in front. Reach and stretch for eight times. Then repeat to the left eight times.

3. Elbow Pulls: Clasp hands behind head and bend at the waist to the right stretching to the count eight times. Repeat on the left side.

4. Twists: Place hands on hips and twist upper body twice to the right and then twist twice to the left. There are two movements to teach "twist". Do a total of sixteen.

5. Wood Chops: Clasp hands together over head, feet shoulder width apart. Swing arms down through legs, bending knees and stretch arms through legs. Then, swing arms back up over head. Do a total of eight.

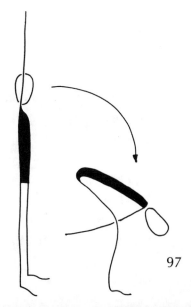

Waist Exercises on the Floor:

1. Waist and Inner Thigh Stretch: Sit up straight on the floor, stomach pulled in, legs stretched open as wide as feels comfortable. Stretch left arm over head to the right and curve right arm to the left in front of you. Gently stretch eight times. Then switch sides and repeat for a total of eight. (Shake out your legs.)

2. Chest-to-Knee Stretch and Walk: Legs stretched open wide, stretch down over right leg, hands on either side of leg. Do eight stretches. Then "walk" your body using your hands, making eight "steps"over to the left leg. Stretch eight times over the left leg. "Walk" back to the right leg and repeat. (Shake out your legs.)

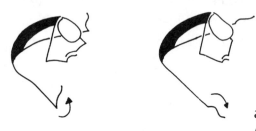

3. Point and Flex: With toes pointed, support the weight of your upper body on your hands. Lean body forward and stretch eight times. Then flex feet and stretch forward eight times. (Shake out your legs.)

4. Inner Thigh Stretch: Sit up straight, stomach pulled in, and bring the soles of your feet together in front of you, pulling

feet as close to your body as is comfortable. Then lean body forward for the stretch. For a gentler stretch, grab toes and lean body forward to each count. Or, for a deeper stretch, alternate arms extended in front of you and push palms forward. do sixteen. (Shake out your legs.)

Abdominals

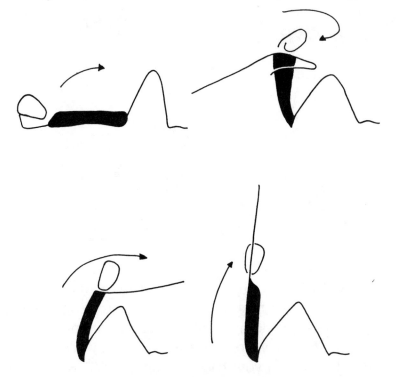

1. Contractions: Lie on back, knees slightly bent. Place hands on legs and sit up halfway, pressing your back into the floor and contracting stomach muscles. Lie back and repeat. Do eight.

2. Sit-ups: Lie on back, knees slightly bent. Begin by sitting up, then twist upper body to the right, come back to center, and lower. Next, sit up, twist upper body to the left, come back to center and lower. Sit up again, stretch arms forward, come back to center and lower. Sit up, stretch arms up to heaven, come back to center and lower. Repeat this series for a total of four times.

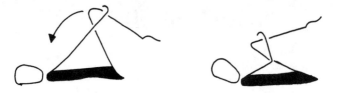

3. Knee Hug: Hug knees tightly to chest for six counts, then hold knees in a relaxed poition for six counts and repeat.

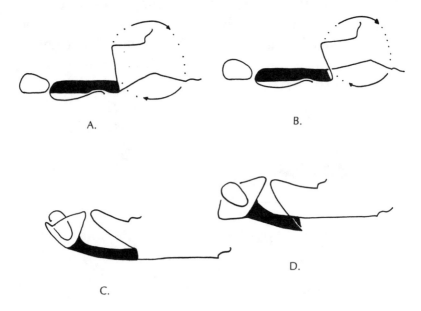

A.

B.

C.

D.

4. Bicycle: Lie on back with hands behind head, and bicycle legs for a total of thirty-two times. Try to keep legs as close to the floor as possible to better work the stomach muscles. If you have a bad back or haven't done any stomach exercises in a while, place your hands under the small of your back for support (A & B). For a more strenuous work out, alternate elbows to your knees (as in C & D).

5. Stomach Stretch: Lie on back, with bent knees to the left and arms to the right over head, count to eight and stretch and release stomach muscles. Then switch sides, knees right and arms left and repeat for eight counts.

6. Seat Walk: Sitting up straight, arms shoulder height in front of you, "walk" your seat forward eight counts and back eight counts and repeat three more times.

7. Hip Rolls: Lie on floor, arms spread shoulder height for support, and bring knees to chest. Roll knees to the right, come center, and roll left. Repeat for a total of four sets.

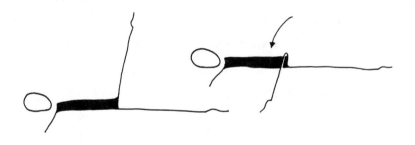

8. Leg Crosses: Lie on back with arms spread shoulder height for support. Raise right leg waist level and cross leg left over body, back up, and lower leg. Repeat with left leg and continue for a total of eight.

Legs and Hips

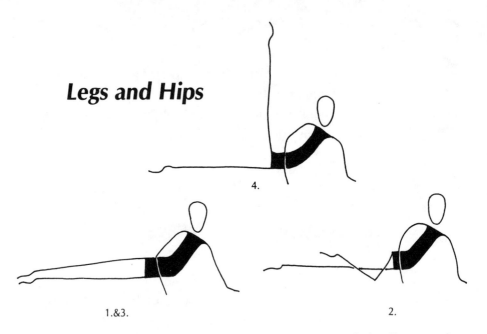

4.

1.&3.

2.

1. Knee In — Leg Lifts: Lie on left side, up on left elbow palms on the floor. Place both legs straight out with stomach pulled in and seat tucked under. Bend right knee into body, extend right leg, lift right leg straight up and lower. These four movements are one set. Do eight sets. Roll over and repeat exercise working the left leg.

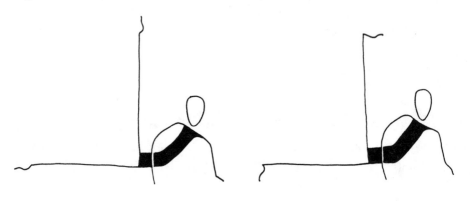

2. Leg Lifts: Lie on left side, up on elbow, palms on the floor, with both legs straight out, point toes and raise and lower right leg eight times. Then flex the foot and raise and lower right leg eight times. Roll over and repeat exercise working the left leg.

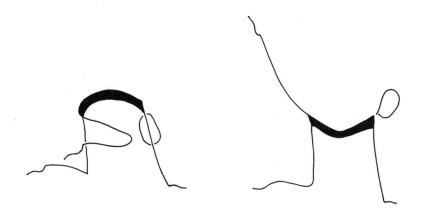

3. Knee to Nose: On hands and knees, bring right knee into chest, pulling head down. Then release leg back out and arch back while lifting head. Repeat for a total of eight times. Then work the left leg eight times.

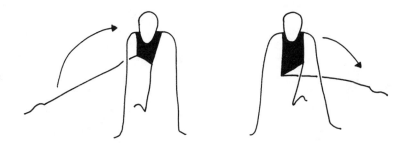

4. Prayer Stretch: Sit back on heels with arms stretched out in front. Next, lean forward and stretch up, supporting yourself on arms while letting the hips fall forward. Do this exercise four times.

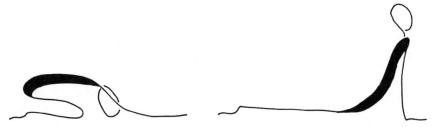

5. Leg Swings: On hands and knees, begin with the right leg out at almost a right angle to your body. Swing right leg to the left across the left leg and repeat. Do eight of these and switch to work the left for a total of eight.

Leg Finale

6. Standing Leg Lifts: Grab a chair, wall or pole, etc., for support, stand up straight, stomach pulled in with the right side of the body facing the chair. Swing the right leg forward and back for eight counts. Then, turn around so that the left side of the body faces the chair, and repeat eight counts with the left leg.

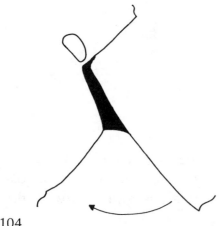

7. Next, face the chair and lift the right leg behind you for eight counts and then work the left leg for eight counts.

A Final Word about Discipline

As you have probably observed upon reading the *Member's Manual*, 3D is a program with various phases which provide sound balance.

You have just finished reading about one—exercise! Ed Haver's encouragement to exercise has no doubt stimulated you to want to tighten that muscle tone through regular exercise.

Another phase, or course—*the diet!* You may discover that being on a diet may trigger some feelings inside of you that may surprise you. The American Diabetic Association diet is the most balanced diet available, and affords you much variety with the exchange program. Even so, just being on a diet and having to account for all you eat can make you angry, frustrated, or even depressed. This is why 3D provides another vital phase—some very positive input!

We believe you will be amazed at how the workbook and the teaching tapes will clarify for you what is happening inside of you emotionally. They will give you encouragement and hope as you discover more about yourself. These down-to-earth, realistic devotional aids will help you not only come face-to-face with you, but also face-to-face with the One who knows and loves you intimately.

From its beginnings, God has combined the understanding of the needs of the body, mind and spirit together in this very unique program. We in 3D are aware that He has raised up the concepts and ideas that you have been reading, and it is only with His help that any of us can even attempt to live disciplined lives.

All the suggestions that are included in these materials have been a part of 3D from the beginning days. If you find that you are only able to handle a few disciplines at a time, express this to your leaders immediately. Then agree together on the parts of the program that you are going to make a commitment to work on. Perhaps after three weeks you can add another discipline and keep taking further steps. *But don't get discouraged.* It is not easy to start all over in reshaping your life by learning how to eat a different way, or how to share a thought or feeling with another individual. It is not easy to sit in a circle and pray for people you hardly know. But it is possible.

Discipleship

Following the Master

ebster's Dictionary defines *discipleship* as one who follows his/her Master.

All 3 "D's" are integral parts of the "3D" program. They compliment one another. Solomon in Ecclesiastes said that a three fold cord is not easily broken. Let's take a brief look at how essential each "D" is to "3D"!

The First "D" in 3D is Diet. Healthy eating will after weeks and months become part of your thinking, and your way of life. Not just for three months, six months or even a year experiment, but hopefully you will benefit from this well-balanced eating and it will be an established lifetime pattern which you enjoy.

Discipline, the Second "D" is one of the tools of God to aid in the breaking of old habits and the establishing of new ones. In accepting disciplines we are propelled toward our goal. When we accept the disciplines of the 3D diet, we move closer to the goal—healthier bodies and loss of weight (if that's what we need). To reach any valuable goal, we have to learn discipline. In 2 Timothy 2:3 Paul speaks about three disciplined disciples—a solider, an athlete and a farmer. The soldier goes to boot camp and undergoes the rigors of training to be a good soldier. The athlete trains to obtain the prize, and the farmer rises early and labors hard to receive the fruit. There are no instant doctors, artists nor instant musicians. They all require rigorous training and discipline. Whatever we practice long enough becomes part of us. Your 3D experience can provide a framework to motivate and assist the learning of personal discipline. Discipline brings liberty.

The Third "D"—Discipleship—is more difficult to define. In John 15:8, Jesus says: "This is to my Father's glory, that you bear much fruit, showing yourselves to be my disciples." (NIV)

Yes, our discipleship is revealed by the fruit we bear. Through the 3D program, we trust you will discover that true spirituality is reality and honesty. That truth frees us to become well integrated persons. Healthy in body, disciplined and able to make good choices. Discipline enables us to choose long range goals above short range satisfactions. The disciplines empower us to follow "the Master"—Jesus. Remarkably fruit thrives and flourishes as we obey and follow Him.

Our goal is Discipleship! Following Jesus Christ through our life. Diet and Discipline are two of the ingredients of Discipleship. God extraordinarily uses them to beckon us on to Discipleship.

We encourage you to use the Resource Materials on the following pages which are available through our 3D office. Keep in touch with us and let us hear from you. It is your thoughts and ideas that help us listen to the Lord for new developments in 3D. Your input is important to us!

Devotional Workbooks

Each of our 3D sessions have a specific thrust which is woven into the devotional workbook and th teaching tapes which we recommend for each session. Let us tell you about each one.

Session One *A New Beginning*

A twelve week session in which the Biblical concept of accountability works itself into the heart of the 3D member.

Here is where you learn to take your dieting seriously. You come to grips with your specific problem—and what it is going to take to resolve it. Everyone's needs in the weight department are different, and you will follow a plan ideally suited to your need. And yet, whether you have ten pounds to lose or a hundred and ten, the key is accountability—to God, to others, and to yourself.

The workbook leads us into a knowledge of what God expects of us in very practical parts of our life. And then shows us how to bring Him into the middle of our problems. Many of us may know the answers in our heads—but have trouble applying them with all our hearts. The daily questions in the workbook will bring the head and heart together.

As we come to know what He expects of us, we become more comfortable with—and desirous of—being accountable to Him. This session also focuses on the importance of sustained prayer—to Him for help, understanding and grace, and for others in the program. For without the power of ongoing prayer any success will almost certainly be temporary and superficial.

You will be challenged to memorize one verse of Scripture each week—a verse well-chosen to help you withstand the inevitable temptations and frustrations that will be in your path on this walk.

Accountability also takes on a very practical form. You will be asked to keep an accurate and honest food diary, and to record in detail the spiritual disciplines which you have agreed to undertake. You will be amazed at what a blessed corrective such a simple act of obedience can be!

Weekly Devotional Themes:

The Lordship of Christ
Why Discipline?
God's Will or My Will?
Learning to Listen
The Blessing of Obedience
Nobody Tells Me What to Do
Those Whom I Love I Reprove
If We Confess Our Sins
Emotions: What to Do With Them
When Light is Darkness
Your Mind: A Battleground
What is Discipleship?

Session Two *The Heart of the Matter*

By this time you will have been part of the 3D program for more than three months. You will have had success in losing weight, you'll have made long-term friends and will have come into a new dimension in your spiritual walk. You'll have learned how to care for others and will have a deeper awareness of the power of prayer.

And you'd like to think that at last the diet aspect of your need is under control.

Well, it may be, but this is the session where you learn there is still lots to learn—about maintenance, plateaus, slow weight loss, and even weight gains that slip in unnoticed. Here is where you learn the lessons that will last a lifetime.

In this twelve-week session we get down to what really motivates us in our hearts. Often we are surprised to find that it is not what we thought. Sometimes, in fact, it comes as a shock—but that is where God smiles and friends help. Learning to identify the root causes of our undisciplined behavior and calling them by name— jealousy, vindictiveness, anger, selfpity, pride, fear—can be tremendously freeing. It is often a painful process, and too frequently we avoid pain by anesthetizing ourselves with food, sleep, busyness— anything that keeps us comfortable.

Being comfortable in our Christian life can be a grave hindrance to spiritual growth. We need to know who we are— and where we need His help. For He *will* help us. We can change. Thousands upon thousands have undergone profound change, spiritually and mentally, as well as physically, in the 3D program.

The practical disciplines of proper diet, exercise, Bible study, prayer and caring for others continue in the session. There is a new dimension of spiritual awareness—and desire to have God in the center of our daily life.

Weekly Devotional Themes:

> The Joy of Being Open
> Learning to Forgive Yourself
> The Hidden Bitter Root
> Won't Somebody Love Me?
> What's Wrong with Being Right?
> Who, Me, Angry?

Why Doesn't Someone Understand?
The Fine Art of Getting Even
Every Day is a New Beginning
Fear: Faith in the Wrong Person—You
Playing God—The Sin of Control
Pressing Toward the Goal

Session Three *Pressing On*

By now you will have become a seasoned veteran of 3D and will be learning what it means to be a Soldier of the Cross. But at this point you'll no doubt be struck with the subtle temptation to let up. Here is where so many defect and drop away. For it is precisely when we have gained a measure of success that we are most vulnerable.

Here is where so many of the 85% of successful dieters become overconfident and ultimately fail. "Frankly, I'm tired of dieting. I've lost the weight I wanted to lose, I'm praying and reading my Bible almost every day, and I simply don't have the time to keep going to meetings and filling out food sheets."

The choice will be yours. In this session the guideline is *responsibility;* you are now responsible for making the right choices. And that choice is to persevere. This twelve-week session challenges us to firmly root and establish the work God has done in us. And now we begin to see the fruit of our obedience overflowing into the lives whom our life touches. For the real test of what has happened in us will be how it blesses others.

But when we have been blessed spiritually—and have been a blessing to others—it is easy to neglect the basic, practical needs which drew us into the program in the first place. And so, these twelve weeks are also a time to re-commit ourselves to the practical side of 3D—eating sensibly, exercising regularly, and being obedient to all the nitty-gritty disciplines which have laid such a good foundation. "It is the little foxes which spoil the vine. . . ."

Weekly Devotional Themes:

> New Lamps for Old
> Learning to Live with Me
> Learning to Live with Others
> Learning to Live Openly
> But it Hurts
> Forgiving One Another
> Perseverance
> The Fork in the Road
> Changing Habit Patterns
> The Peace of God

His Mercy Endures
Where Do We Go From Here?

Session Four *Along the King's Highway*

As you have already discovered, 3D is so much more than a weight control program! It has been teaching you to see with God's eyes— and with His compassion. As you begin to realize how little you truly know about what motivates you, you come to a new under-standing of God's patience and mercy with you— of His enduring love for you.

He wants you to change, to become more conformed to the image of His Son. But He also knows that you cannot, unless you truly want to. And so, by His Spirit, He is drawing you gradually into a deep-er spirituality—until ultimately, nothing is more important than pleas-ing Him.

This fourth devotional workbook offers key assistance on that jour-ney. With its daily Bible readings, questions, and weekly Scripture verse to memorize, it will clarify and crystallize the progress you are making along the King's Highway. It can be used in a support group, as a church or prayer group's Bible Study, or as a personal or family devotional.

If you will do each lesson faithfully for the twelve assigned weeks, they will seal what God has been showing you, so that you will easily recall them, in times of great need.

One thing: if you are willing to be transparently honest as you answer the questions, He will give you fresh insights, even as you write.

Weekly Devotional Themes:

> Baby Steps
> Side Steps
> Back Steps
> Traps and Pitfalls
> Wayward Wanderings
> Road Blocks
> Growing Weary on the Road
> Resting Places
> Heeding the Signs
> Uphill, Downhill
> Traveling Light
> Walking with Jesus

Session Five *Heart Beats*

God is very interested in the condition of our hearts, physically and spiritually. He wants us to know the importance of keeping our hearts in good condition. This session helps you examine the important elements involved in having and maintaining a healthy heart.

"You made us for yourself, and our hearts are restless until they rest in you." (St. Augustine)

Weekly Devotional Themes:

> The Examined Heart
> The Troubled Heart
> The Best of Rooms
> The Uncommitted Heart
> The Hungry Heart
> A Wandering Heart
> The Broken Heart
> The Heart Has its Reasons
> The Steadfast Heart
> A Heart Filled with Gratitude
> The Awakened Heart
> The Satisfied Heart